"For the most part, rats and journalists write true crime books. This book is not one of those pieces of garbage. If you own a rat book, throw it away. It's not worth the paper it's printed on."

- **Johnny Toracio**

"In this life, you grow up with your friends deceiving, stealing, cheating, lying and manipulating, then eventually you turn on each other.

There is no honor among thieves. You're only as good as your last envelope full of cash.

Today's bosses will call you their best friend, but be late with an envelope, and see what happens. It doesn't matter how much you brought them in the past – even if it was hundreds of thousands of dollars.

These days it's all about greed and money.

You can argue greed and money are what drive a legitimate business.

However, in business, you don't fear for your life, and you don't carry two handguns to protect yourself.

I spent many years in the Salerno Crime Family of New York City, and now I am out.

Everything is different now, and my life will never be what it used to be.

This is my story."

– **Carlo Juliano**

THE LIFE THAT CHOSE ME

I heard a gunshot and thud hit the ground behind me. I turned around and saw my dad on his back with a blank stare.

A cold shudder ran down my spine as I lost my breath.

In a few minutes, my life changed forever. A mob hit man murdered my dad on a public street in broad daylight.

Earlier that year, my mom overdosed on heroin.

At 14 years old, I was orphaned and homeless.

It was October 10, 2009.

In the aftermath, I felt scared, afraid, anxious, rejected, alone, unloved, and depressed.

I stole food, and slept in unlocked parked cars on the neighborhood streets.

I figured out how to survive on my own.

Every now and then, I woke up in the middle of the night in tears staring at the moon and stars wondering, "What happened to my life?"

Two months later, it was the night before Christmas. I wandered the streets aimlessly trying to distract myself by looking at decorations in shop windows.

I walked past a bar owned by Johnny Toracio several times.

He sat at a table inside alone near the front window looking out at the street.

He was an important person in the neighborhood.

Each time I passed, my grief-stricken eyes met his thoughtful gaze.

A few minutes before midnight, he opened the front door intercepting my path and calmly lit his cigarette.

He took a deep drag and squinted his eyes.

December 24, 2009

JOHNNY: Hey kid, I knew your father. Where are you going?

CARLO: I don't know.

JOHNNY: Come in here for a moment. It is cold outside. How are you doing?

CARLO: I'm alright.

JOHNNY: Where are you sleeping tonight?

CARLO: Nowhere.

JOHNNY: I'm getting ready to leave. You're sleeping here. This place is yours tonight. I'll grab you some blankets and a pillow.

Here are the keys to the back door. Leave the front door locked. There is food in the bar fridge.

I'll check on you tomorrow afternoon. I have to visit my ex-wife's house and kid in the morning.

If you need to leave, go through the back, and lock up.

There is a mattress in the room on the right in the back.

Here are the remotes for the televisions above the bar.

I got to go, see you kid.

Why are you smiling so big?

CARLO: I met you.

JOHNNY: You met me? Hey, what are you doing for dinner tomorrow night?

CARLO: Nothing, I'm wide open.

JOHNNY: You want to come to my mother's house? I'm heading over there.

End of conversation dated December 24, 2009

His human compassion saved me that night. The next day, I woke up, turned on the TV, made myself sandwiches, and drank sodas.

Johnny came by in the afternoon.

I couldn't hold back another big smile when I saw him.

I remember sitting at my first holiday dinner with Johnny's family, which was now my family.

For the first time in a long time, I felt like I belonged, like I was wanted, like somebody in this world cared about me.

Johnny gave me a job at his bar cleaning and taking messages for him. He set me up with my own apartment a couple weeks later.

I was on my way up in the world.

THE CHANDELIER

Johnny embodied charisma and walked around like he owned the world with his back straight and a self-assured smile. When he spoke, it was like, there was God standing right over me.

In the afternoons during the week, Johnny's bar was usually empty, and he would drop by and talk about random topics.

When we talked, he let his guard down and had a regular conversation. I enjoyed these talks and learned a lot about the criminal lifestyle.

December 30, 2009

JOHNNY: Let the dummies do home burglary. You're too smart to get caught up in that.

CARLO: Have you ever done it?

JOHNNY: Years ago, I did. I got out of it because, on the hierarchy of things I could do as a wiseguy, I learned home burglary is on the bottom for low-life scumbags.

There is no honor in robbing a man's home.

It is more respectable in my book to rob a company, a bank, a store, a warehouse, a truck full of merchandise, the government or other places.

Do you want to know what really bothered me? When the people I robbed were bigger thieves than me.

One time, I robbed the house of the Mayor of Clifton, New Jersey.

I went through his house, and all I found was cheap garbage.

The Mayor bought his wife costume jewelry like what you would find sitting on a dollar sale rack next to a display of used mariachi outfits at the local flea market on a Saturday morning.

There was only one good find.

I discovered a ring that appeared to have a large diamond in the center over three carats.

Afterwards, my jeweler took a look at it, shook his head, and told me it was cubic zirconia.

I ran the ring under water for 30 seconds. It turned green.

I was furious.

The ring was pewter and spray-painted gold.

I threw it away.

That isn't the end of the story. A couple days later in the morning, I had my morning cup of coffee while I read the newspaper.

On an inside page where the local police blotter describes recent crimes, there it was.

The headline in bold read, "Burglars steal $120,000 in jewelry, art, electronics and furniture from Clifton Mayor's home."

Can you believe it?

The Mayor wanted the insurance money, so he lied about what was stolen from his home.

I didn't take any art, electronics or furniture like the headline said.

What a crook.

People believe our politicians lie and cheat, and now I can see why.

I became so frustrated, I almost called the cops to dispute the Mayor's claims, but then I realized who is going to believe me, the burglar?

What makes it worse is if I was ever caught later on down the line and charged for the Mayor's home burglary, I would be charged for the amount of his insurance claim, and not for what I actually stole!

Maybe I should have kept the green ring.

At the trial, I could have told the judge in my own defense, "I submit as evidence this green pewter ring to refute the Mayor's property loss claims, and I request all charges against me be dropped effective immediately!"

CARLO: I understand your point. What was the most cash you ever found in a house?

JOHNNY: This is a good one. My partner said he heard about a Wall Street guy who was a chronic gambler and bought tons of cocaine from the Salerno family. The guy always paid for his coke and the bets he made with big stacks of cash.

My partner put two and two together and realized this Wall Street guy had to be holding piles of cash in his condo.

We did some research and mapped out the guy's routine. When his place was empty, we hit the condo. We rummaged through every drawer and turned the place completely upside down looking for the cash. We couldn't find any of it. I told my partner that I think he led us on a wild goose chase. He got defensive and took a swing at me.

We started wrestling in the bedroom bumping into furniture.

He threw me into one of the dressers, and I knocked it over.

A drawer opened and landed upside down on the floor exposing a brown envelope taped to the underside of it.

We stopped wrestling and staggered to our feet.

I opened the envelope and there was $20,000 cash inside.

The dresser had nine total drawers. I checked under the other eight drawers and there was an envelope under each one.

We couldn't believe our eyes when we saw $20,000 was under each one. On top of that, one of the drawers had 30 neatly folded handkerchiefs, and inside each handkerchief was $500 in cash.

But that wasn't the only dresser in the room. The guy had a wife.

On her side of the room, there was another identical nine drawer dresser.

We smirked at each other.

We think we have another gold mine waiting for us, but when we tear it apart, we found nothing.

Let me ask you, why do you think we found nothing?

Husbands always hide cash from their wives.

The key lesson here is if there is ever any cash to be had in house, it is always hiding in the husband's stuff.

CARLO: Interesting. One thing I've wondered about is how does a burglar keep a dog from attacking him if he encounters one in a house?

JOHNNY: Spaghetti and meatballs, you bring a plastic bag of it with you.

After you kick in the front door, you wait and see if a dog comes charging toward you.

You have the bag ready and dump it on the floor.

You're immediately the dog's best friend, and while it is eating, you go to the refrigerator and look for other things to feed it like leftovers, pork chops, chicken, steaks, or anything edible.

After the dog eats everything, no matter how big or mean it originally was when you walked in the door, it will look up at you with a friendly look, go find a place to lie down, exhale a satisfied "arf", and take a nap.

At that point, the house is yours.

I used to get repulsed by what I found going through other people's things.

I learned that people are freaks, especially the ones with large houses and lots of stuff. When I went into the master bedroom, I would find sex toys in the wife's panty drawer, dirty pictures of the wife in the husband's underwear drawer, and a box of pornographic videos behind the husband's coats hanging the master closet.

CARLO: What kind of stuff was best to rob?

JOHNNY: It was always jewelry because it is small, portable, highly valuable, and easy to sell. For the bigger stuff like televisions, rare china, art or furniture, I would take those only if there was a car in the garage with the keys in it. If I did, then I loaded the car up with as much stuff as possible, opened the garage, and drove away.

Otherwise, I filled up a pillowcase with the jewelry, hid it under my coat, left the house out the front door, and calmly walked down the street to my car parked a few blocks away.

The best houses for jewelry fell into two categories.

The first category was by the type of car parked in the garage. If it was a flashy car, like a red Cadillac with bright gold trim and white leather interior, then there would be lots of fake jewelry in the collection.

If the car parked in the garage was conservative, like a Ford, Buick or Chevy four-door sedan, then the jewelry would be real and pretty good.

The second category of houses for the best jewelry was from people who had what I call "fuck you" money.

These were people who had huge egos and used their money to buy things for their homes which were over the top and completely unnecessary in order to tell the world, "I can afford to buy this and you can't!"

When I would hear about these type of people being robbed or read about them in the paper, I imagined the burglars teaching the owners a valuable lesson about the consequences of having too big of an ego and being too much of a show off.

As strange as it may sound, I looked at it as the burglars did the community a favor by serving these people a slice of humble pie.

Personally, I have a problem with people who flaunt their possessions shamelessly to satisfy an ego.

Although I never fault anyone for wanting to own nice things because who doesn't want to own nice things?

I like to own nice things.

The difference between me and them is I don't flaunt my stuff.

A few years ago, I robbed a house that felt like I entered a roman palace with a massive white marble foyer and tall columns from floor to ceiling.

The columns surrounded a fountain with the statue of a topless woman in the center.

Above the statue, hanging from the ceiling was a massive, eight-foot-tall custom chandelier consisting of thousands of small pieces of glass. The light magnificently reflected off each piece of glass creating tiny rainbows.

It was a work of art.

I marveled at it for a moment, and then I tried to figure out why the chandelier was shaped in such an odd way.

The chandelier was in the shape of a cylinder six-foot-long and three feet wide with a rounded top.

At the bottom of the cylinder were two three-foot-wide globes next to each other and butted up against it.

Then, I stepped back, thought for a moment, and realized the chandelier was in the shape of a large glass penis with two glass balls.

The owner of the house had it right there in the front foyer for everyone who entered his house to admire.

The owner was saying, "Look, my cock is bigger than yours could ever possibly be!"

If the owner had enough money to commission an artist to create such an obscene, custom chandelier like this, then I couldn't wait to see what he had waiting for me in his wife's jewelry collection.

Was my intuition correct?

Yeah, it was one of my best scores.

There was $250,000 worth of jewelry, but I could only get $62,500 for it.

CARLO: Why couldn't you get more money?

JOHNNY: Everybody wants a deal, especially the jeweler who is buying my stolen merchandise.

The jeweler wants to unload it quickly on a customer with cash who is looking for a deal.

Nobody wants to pay much for stolen merchandise.

The numbers worked out where my jeweler planned to sell $250,000 worth of jewelry for $125,000. He gave me half the $125,000 amount, which was $62,500, and he kept the other half.

CARLO: Did you try to take the custom chandelier?

JOHNNY: I left the chandelier right where it was. Who would buy such a thing?

And if I did find a guy who wanted to buy it, would he have a foyer big enough to display it?

Let's say the foyer was big enough.

My next question would be what kind of a wife would allow such a thing in her home?

As a joke, I thought about removing the two glass globes at the bottom of the chandelier, and leaving just the shaft hanging from the ceiling, but I didn't follow through with it.

Toward the end of my short career in home burglary, I only robbed houses with "fuck you" money.

I justified my actions by convincing myself I was providing the owner a lesson in humility at no charge.

When my justification wore thin, I stopped.

CARLO: I understand. Did you ever get busted during or after a robbery?

JOHNNY: One time, I came real close. My partner and I were in a house and loaded a van the owner had in the garage with every possible thing we could fit into it to the point where the van's rear end side doors would barely close.

There was only room left inside for him and me to squeeze into the driver and passenger seats.

We made our getaway and drove carefully out of the neighborhood.

At the first traffic light, it was red, and we stopped in the left turn lane.

As we were sitting at the light, a cop car was flying down the highway at 100 miles per hour with his lights flashing and sirens blowing.

As he turned, his car's rear end swung out and clipped our rear bumper.

The cop slammed on his brakes, his tires screeched, and he ran over to our van.

He apologized for hitting us and asked us if we were ok. Then, he told us to pullover on the side of the road, and wait there until he returned from a burglary in progress. We took off as soon as he left.

End of Conversation Dated December 30, 2009

Even though many other kids my age I knew burglarized homes, I never did. What I learned from speaking to others besides Johnny who did home burglaries is they were addicted to the rush from doing it. However, they didn't get away with it. They were all eventually caught and went to jail for it.

WORK AND HEALTH

On this afternoon, Johnny called the bar and asked me to pick him up at a nice hotel in Manhattan. When I arrived, he looked fatigued like he was still blasted from the prior night.

He was waiting outside talking to a bellhop and lighting a cigarette.

One of the coolest things I remember about Johnny was how he lit a cigarette with one hand. First, he put the cigarette in his mouth, and then pulled out the matches. He held the matchbox with two outer fingers, and struck the match between his thumb and first finger.

He careened toward the car.

January 7th, 2010

JOHNNY: Hey kid, thanks for dropping by.

CARLO: Is everything alright?

JOHNNY: Absolutely. I never felt better. I just paid my hotel bill. Can you believe I barely had enough cash to cover it? Me, Johnny Toracio, almost broke in the middle of the city. It is all because last night I lost a big chunk of cash on a cab ride back to the hotel.

I didn't realize it until I woke up this morning and checked my pockets. The cab fare last night was small, maybe seven dollars. I was lit up on booze and some other stuff.

I had a beautiful girl with me, and I wasn't paying attention. I counted out ten bills, gave them to the cab driver and said keep the change.

I was focused on taking my girl into the hotel and getting to the room as quick as possible. You know what I mean? Anyways, the problem was the bills I gave to the driver were not one dollar bills.

I was out of my mind.

I gave the driver ten one hundred dollar bills.

He cleaned me out. That's why I called you to pick me up.

CARLO: You gave the cab driver $1,000 in cash?

JOHNNY: Can you believe the son of a bitch didn't give me back any change?

Maybe he didn't know. Maybe he did.

On second thought, nobody misses out on noticing that kind of money.

Who would miss that kind of money?

It was a nice holiday bonus for him courtesy of me. Ho, ho, ho. I'm Santa.

The next time I see him he'll owe me a free ride, or I should say the next hundred times. If only I could remember what he looked like, I might kill him the next time I see him.

I'm only joking. I don't mind it too much.

It does make me feel good to help a guy out.

CARLO: Cab drivers, how much does one of them make a year?

JOHNNY: I don't know, maybe $50,000, if they are lucky. I know it is tough to live on whatever they make. They are blue collar guys. They live paycheck to paycheck.

I have respect for anyone who gets up every day, goes to a regular job, and works hard to earn a living. These guys are the backbone of our country.

I know I couldn't do it. I wouldn't have a clue on how to control my spending or live on a budget. I don't even know how much I spend or how much I make a year. The money comes in and then it goes out.

When I need more, I go get it.

CARLO: You couldn't live on $50,000 a year?

JOHNNY: Ha! My bar tabs are at least $50,000 a year!

It would be impossible, not with my expenses, and not with my life.

I go out every night.

It's expensive. I like to enjoy myself.

Who doesn't?

Add weed, cocaine and other drugs I enjoy to the drink total, and now I am at well over a $100,000 every year.

And that's just the beginning. I go to Las Vegas or Atlantic City twice a month and each trip costs me around $5,000 for gambling, food, room and drinks at the casino.

Sometimes, I come back from these trips worn out, and I need a vacation from the vacation! You have no idea.

Don't get me wrong, I know I have a problem.

I bet $500 a weekend on NFL games, college football games, NBA, college basketball, hockey, and the list never stops.

I lose more than I win.

Sometimes, I will bet on both sides of a game.

I bet the Giants will win, and I also bet they will lose, just to know I win one of the bets no matter how the game turns out.

It all adds up fast.

Do the math for me. What's my expense total so far?

CARLO: $244,000.

JOHNNY: Ok, let's keep going. There are other entertainment expenses.

I love going out to a nice dinner every night.

I don't like cooking at home. It's too lonely. I like being around other people.

At several restaurants, I have my own table, and I know the owners. I'm addicted to attending the live sporting events we have here for the Knicks, Giants, Jets, Rangers, Yankees, and Mets. How many cities have two football teams and two baseball teams?

We have the best shows and best concerts in the world. We have Broadway and Radio City Music Hall. I attend as many games and shows as I can.

I feel like I am missing out if I don't. Life is happening all around me and I need to be a part of it.

I would guess this all costs another $4,000 a month, round it off to $50,000 a year. Where are we at on the total so far?

CARLO: $294,000.

JOHNNY: I can't forget the women. Oh, the women! I need variety. I tried being married. It didn't work for me.

How could it work for me? I can't be faithful to one woman.

With Al's mother, I tried. I put her through hell.

I'm lucky Al doesn't remember most of the tough times I put his mother through when he was a baby.

I can't get married again. I can't put another woman through that.

I have a problem with commitment. I'm not normal. At least I recognize it.

The women I date are a part of my entertainment expenses I already described. I might take a date with me on a trip, out to dinner, or to a show.

I get so jealous of the women I date. I am dating this girl. She is 21, still young and wild.

I thrive on always watching her, catching her doing things she shouldn't, like a cat and mouse game.

No one can believe how possessive and jealous I am of her.

I have guys all over the city and in my hangouts that are my eyes and ears watching her when she is out with her friends.

If someone is acting inappropriately to her, one of my guys always informs me like from a couple weeks ago.

FM's is a Manhattan dance club where the young crowd goes. I like to hang out in these kinds of places. They allow me to still act like I am young, and pretend I am young. I think a part of me never grew up.

One night, I heard one of the Salerno guys was there drinking, taking ecstasy, smoking weed, and doing a two-step shuffle with my girl on the dance floor.

I waited until after the club closed. To verify the story, I watched the security camera tapes.

I sent a message that I needed to see the Salerno guy.

I confronted him. He had no idea what it was about.

He lamented, "I was wasted. I had no idea she was your girl."

I commanded him to stay away from her and walked away.

The following week I received another tip about my girl acting up at the same club.

For that night, she had told me she planned to have a quiet night at a girlfriend's house.

I hate when a woman lies to me!

I wanted to catch her in the act and went to the club. In the packed club, I had trouble finding her.

I approached the DJ's booth, put my .357 magnum under the DJ's chin, and told him to announce the club was closed.

The crowd headed to the exit single file.

I found her, grabbed her arm, and we left the club. She knew she did wrong.

The paradox of me is I expect complete loyalty from my women, but I am terrible at it.

Let me get back to my expenses.

What we've talked about so far are just my expenses for entertainment. This doesn't begin to include my regular everyday expenses and bills like a home mortgage, home repairs, electric, gas, water, and cable. That's another $10,000 a month.

Then, I need to add personal expenses like clothing.

I like to look sharp. I wear tailored Italian suits, expensive ties and handmade Italian shoes. They are more comfortable than regular clothes.

Take a glance at these gold cuff links I have on today. Feel them, they're heavy. They cost over $1,800 because there is a lot of real gold in them!

I spend too much on looking sharp. I have a huge wardrobe.

Do I really need so many clothes? But then I ask myself, who doesn't like to look nice when they go out?

Why shouldn't I be able to look nice? I can't help it. You see?

Then, I buy food for the house. Half of the fresh stuff I buy goes bad before I eat it like the fruits and vegetables, and the meats when I forget to freeze them. I end up throwing the spoiled stuff away. It's wasteful. I'm not home enough to eat it all.

Then, there's dry cleaning. Everything I wear is dry cleaned.

Do I need to have everything dry cleaned including my drawers, socks and undershirts? No, but I like the crisp creases in everything, and the clothes feel cleaner than when I just wash them at the house. Plus, it's easier. The clothes come back folded, on hangers, and organized.

You picked up my clothes from the cleaners. You could probably estimate that expense better than me.

Lastly, there are my cars.

Do I need to trade them in every year for new ones? No.

Do I like shopping for a new car? Absolutely.

Do I like the smell of a new car? Of course.

Do I like to worry about car repairs? No, that's why I get new cars.

Could I get by on one car instead of three? Yes, but who wants to just get by? Especially, if you don't have to? I don't.

You see what I mean? The depreciation alone on the cars must kill me!

I forgot my cleaning lady. I like a clean house, but I don't have the time to clean it. I have better things to do with my time. I guess that's an excuse because I really don't want to clean it. I need someone to do the cleaning for me. You see?

These expenses easily total another $100,000 a year. I'm terrible, right?

CARLO: Who wouldn't want to live your life? What a life!

Who wouldn't be envious?

You have good reasons for why you do what you do. Back to adding up the expenses, the total is $525,000.

JOHNNY: Wow, I never added it all up. Those are just the expenses I am pulling off the top of my head. There are others.

I have unexpected expenses when I go out that I can't predict. Last week, I took my crew to a strip club. We had a table in a corner surrounded by 10 beautiful women partying and dancing with us.

Then, all of the sudden, a famous rapper sat down with four of his friends at a table next to us.

Our girls recognized and waved at him.

He flashed them a stack of $100 bills and invited them over to his table.

The women left us.

The rapper broke up my party!

To get my girls back, I walked out to my car, grabbed $25,000 in cash from the glove compartment, and stormed back in the club.

It started raining $100 bills at my table.

All the women ran back over to me.

I yelled to the rapper, "This is my club! Get out of here, you jerkoffs!"

Now back to my original point.

Why would I go to work at a regular job to make fifty grand a year?

A regular job wouldn't come near covering my expenses. It would be a waste of my time and too much of a headache.

Also, I would be miserable in a regular job.

I like my life. I'm happy. My life isn't perfect, but it's my life.

CARLO: How about last night. Did you go out and meet anybody?

JOHNNY: Yeah, I had a good time. I met a girl at O'Shea's bar near Times Square. She was beautiful, tall, great body, and long curly hair.

She looked Italian and wore a silk dress that fit her like a glove. She was out with three of her friends. They looked as good as she did.

Let me tell you, there is nothing harder to do than pull a girl away from her friends when they are all out together.

Girls are loyal to one another. They stick together. If one of them meets a guy, then they all need to meet a guy.

Guys are different. If a group of guys go out, they have no loyalty to one another if one of them meets a girl. If one guy hooks up for the night, then everybody is happy for him. If all of them hook up, then that is even better. You see?

I love a challenge. I thrive on it. We were dancing and having a good time. I made her laugh. I sensed she liked me.

One problem was her three friends were at the bar talking, and my girl kept looking over at them. I could tell she was feeling guilty because she was spending time with me and not her friends. I sensed she wanted to spend the night with me.

I looked around the place and noticed three guys at the other end of the bar across from her friends. I thought they were perfect matches for her friends. My girl excused herself to the restroom.

I had an idea. I went over to the three guys and made a deal with them.

I told them the three lovely young ladies at the other end of the bar are for sale.

CARLO: For sale?

JOHNNY: (chuckles) I told them the ladies are for sale at a big discount of $75 each for the night, and the guys can pay the ladies directly after services rendered.

I guess you might say I pimped out my girl's friends?

CARLO: What did the guys do?

JOHNNY: The guys approached the ladies and talked to them.

The guys thought they were dealing with a sure thing.

Their confidence must have appeared to have that extra boost needed which women find so attractive.

By the time my girl came out of the restroom, her friends were occupied.

My girl had no more guilt, and she was mine for the rest of the night.

CARLO: What happened with her three friends?

JOHNNY: Up until the time her friends left, I kept looking over at her friends to see if they had slapped the guys faces upon discovery of what I had put together without their knowledge or approval.

Her friends would be mad, right? What woman wouldn't be?

Luckily for me it worked out.

Her friends left holding hands with the guys before my girl and I did.

Do I think her friends hooked up with the three guys? Who knows?

Can you imagine what happened at the end of the night if they did?

The guys pull out their wallets to pay each girl $75? The girls might think, "Is this a joke?"

Worse yet, the girls might think, "Is this all I'm worth?"

Then, the girls would reach for the nearest metal object and start swinging at the guys! Watch out!

I have another story about a one-night stand.

She was a wild one. It was early in the morning when I woke up, and she was still asleep.

I picked up my phone, and noticed 22 missed calls from the same number.

Who would call me that many times in one night?

I played the first voicemail and heard a man yell, "You are an asshole; you are with my wife!"

I hung up, as she awoke from hearing her husband's voice.

I told her, "Husband? You never mentioned a husband!"

She reached to hug me, "I don't want him. I want you."

I asked rhetorically, "Oh really, you want me? You just met me! I've only known you for one night. No, no, no, this is wrong. I don't mess with another man's wife. How in the world did your husband get my number?!"

She paused for a moment and confessed, "I guess I called him at the dance club last night."

I howled, "You called him with my phone?! Are you nuts?!"

Then, my phone rang and the voice on the other line bellowed, "Am I talking to the guy who is with my wife?"

I backpedaled, "Look pal, I had no idea she was your wife. I picked her up on the corner and I'll drop her off at the corner where I found her. I don't want her. She's yours!"

He wailed, "Where are you at? I know guys from the union. I fly somebody else's flag; you understand? You are going to get your ass kicked."

This was when I tried to ruffle his feathers, "Hold on pal. I fly someone else's flag too! I am at the corner of 75th and 101st every afternoon. You are welcome to come out there anytime. I am going to drop your wife off and that is it for me."

Three days later, the same girl called asking me to get together.

I told her, "Are you nuts?!"

Hey, do you know where you are taking me?

CARLO: You mentioned a friend of yours in Queens?

JOHNNY: Yeah, he lives near my bar. We have a while before we get there with this traffic.

He just got out of the joint after doing his second bid.

CARLO: What does a "bid" mean?

JOHNNY: A "bid" means his second prison term. He used to rob banks. The next time he gets caught doing that, the judge will give him at least 30 years.

Three strikes and you are out.

The feds don't play around at that point and label him a career criminal.

He is 52 years old. He would be in his eighties when he got out of jail again.

His goal in life now is not to die in jail, which means he is retired.

I remember when he used to rob banks, he looked at it as a regular job.

He used to say, "There is no room for error in my work. If other people screw up at their legitimate jobs, then they get fired or reprimanded. If I screw up, then I go to jail for over 10 years or I get shot.

When I got into this, others told me the odds of getting away with robbing a bank my first time was 80%. I thought those odds were pretty good.

I felt supercharged the first time I got away with it. I kept doing it - that was my demise.

Eventually, the odds stacked up against me and I got caught."

As he kept doing it, besides being caught by the cops, he worried about jealousy and greed from friends and family.

When he bought luxurious cars and lived in lavish places with his bank money, he knew some people might get jealous.

It is human nature.

No one ever gets ratted on by a stranger.

It is always by someone they know.

He never figured out who ratted on him to the cops.

With the money, it was like he painted a bull's eye on his back for anyone to shoot. That's just the way it is.

Within six months of buying his new Bentley, he was locked up in prison.

18 months ago, he was released on probation after ten years locked up.

He walked into a cigar bar, said hello to an old friend who was a wiseguy and under surveillance by the Feds.

Since that friend was also on probation, he was supposed to report the "hello" to his probation officer.

He didn't.

The Feds surveying him did.

The judge sent him back to jail for a year.

Who needs that?

Then, it took my friend forever to be released from prison because he was on medical hold for six months past his official prison release date.

This is because if the Bureau of Prisons deems a person not healthy enough to be released for medical reasons at the end of his sentence, they can keep him in jail in order to fix him up.

As a result, they had prison doctors do the operations he needs, and then they monitored his recovery.

They needed to keep him because his health was a mess. When he was out on the street, he never exercised and smoked incessantly.

As most would expect, he developed health problems and needed a quadruple bypass.

The prison doctors told him his heart was a ticking time bomb.

Also, he did cocaine for years and trashed his kidneys. He needed at least one new kidney because it only functioned at 25%.

The doctors needed to get in there and replace it. In addition, he was overweight.

I heard from others who saw him already that he looks great, he's in shape and he lost a lot of weight.

CARLO: Let me get this straight. Your friend abused his body before he went to jail. He might have known about his health problems or he might not.

He may have put it off like a lot of people might do for as long as possible due to the high expense and discomfort of having surgery.

But, in the case of your friend, he could be viewed as lucky. He went to jail, and the government paid the bill for getting him healthy again with the quadruple bypass, the new kidney and other stuff.

JOHNNY: Yeah, it's the U.S. taxpayer who foots the bill for his surgeries. The same taxpayer as the cab driver we discussed earlier who lives paycheck to paycheck, on maybe $50,000 a year.

Do you think the cab driver could afford the same operations as my friend or be able to take the needed time off work to recover from the surgery? No way.

That is why I believe that jail saved my friend's life. Is this a great country or what?

CARLO: God forbid our country let unhealthy criminals out of jail. To do so might slow down their return to criminal activities.

Didn't you once tell me over half of the guys that get out of prison end up going back?

JOHNNY: Yeah, and the other half doesn't get caught.

I'm joking.

Actually, it depends.

For most guys, jail is a revolving door. For others, it isn't.

I look at jail as a sabbatical for us wiseguys. It is a vacation. It's a break from our crazy life on the streets. Whether or not we realize it, we need the break.

Jail gives us time to get healthy, workout, lose some weight, relax, get our minds right, and address any health issues we may have. This is so when we get out of jail, we can get back to our lives doing what we do.

Wiseguys have their own section together in every jail across the country. We have access to everything: wine, sausages, cheeses, cakes, pizzas, cell phones, and computers. I used to keep $5,000 in my locker to bribe the guards to bring me whatever I needed.

Wiseguys eat the best food in jail.

Sunday dinner was the focal point of the week.

The bosses hosted extravagant Sunday evening meals with antipasto, fresh bread, olive oil, freshly grated parmesan cheese, four meat courses, and several dessert choices.

We used the large ovens in the kitchen to make the meals and bring them to our rooms.

There was lots of wine to drink and phones available to call loved ones.

We converted one of the rooms into a dining area for the twelve of us.

Our cook stayed up all night on Saturdays to make the meatballs, the sauces, the dessert, everything. Other nights of the week, he used to make our favorite dish called Ollie-O. People used to make Ollie-O during the depression because it was cheap, but it was "oh so" delicious.

He first smashed the garlic in a separate pan. He added olive oil to the garlic and cooked it until a golden brown. Then, he cooked the macaroni only to a point where it was slightly hard, which is when he poured the oil and garlic over it, and stirred in freshly ground black pepper. Lastly, he added finely chopped pancetta, which was either a prosciutto or salami.

The only hard part about prison was dealing with the verbal abuse doled out by the old bosses to the young guys coming up from the families.

They used to say things like, "you're a no good rat, I can't believe I vouched for you. I can't believe someone would put a button on you."

A button means you're a made guy.

One time it got so bad for our cook that he didn't come to the table for a couple days.

The boss sent a guy over to his room to let him know that the boss teased him because he really liked him. When the cook returned, the boss asked, "Where have you been? On vacation?"

When a wiseguy goes to jail, he gets treated a lot better than when a regular guy goes to jail.

We own the place. We are like celebrities in the criminal world, especially around young guys who don't have a background from a legitimate crime family.

They aspire to be young gangsters, but they have no idea what it means. These young guys never learned respect.

For example, one day in the dining area, I minded my own business to sit down and eat my lunch.

A kid about 20 years old stood next to me with his tray of food.

I looked up at him with a look on my face like, "What the fuck are you doing invading my space?"

He pointed down at me, smiled, and shouted to his friends seated at the next table, "I'm going to eat my lunch today with a real gangster!"

On the streets, this guy wouldn't be allowed to talk to me!

What's wrong with this kid?

Is he out of his mind?

He didn't know the rules.

Inside jail, the kid has access to important guys like me.

I calmly told him, "Get the fuck out of here."

Guys like him have no courage and heart.

They are not standup guys.

When they face any type of adversity, they whine, complain or rat. I stay away from them.

In jail, you can be anyone you want to be.

Would you believe there are a few young guys in every jail walking around telling everyone they are a big shot in one of the New York families?

I'll tell you a story.

At the beginning of my last bid, I heard about one of these guys.

I got excited and thought it would be great to hang out with someone from back home.

I introduced myself. We hit it off, and had some laughs. I asked him, "Who's your boss?"

Immediately, he clammed up.

He didn't say another word. He looked physically sick.

Sweat ran down his forehead, the whole thing. He realized I had a button.

I thought nothing of it, and told him it was nice to meet him.

Right after I return to my room there is a call on the speaker, "Mr. Toracio, please report to the guard desk."

I'm thinking, oh boy, what did I do now?

The guard takes me to the warden's office where a special investigations officer is sitting with the warden.

They told me to sit down.

The officer starts yelling at me, "Toracio, you don't bring any of your mobster shit here! If you do, I'll ship you to the toughest place the Bureau of Prisons has in Alaska! I'm watching your ass!"

I tell him I understood, and they let me go back to my room.

Later, I find out the guy was not in any family.

He worked in a union and ratted on some guys in one of the families.

I guess I spooked him after I introduced myself and he went running to the guards fearful of his safety.

He was nothing but a fucking, low-life rat.

If he would have just kept his mouth shut, and not lied about being a mobster big shot, I never would have sought him out in the first place.

CARLO: Understood, what about the beds? Don't you sleep on concrete beds in jail?

JOHNNY: Where did you hear that nonsense?
We sleep on mattresses handmade by the other
inmates. They take 30 soft new pillows and knit
them into one large mattress that feels like you
are sleeping on a cloud.

A lot of wiseguys say their beds in jail are better
than the ones they have at home.

CARLO: Jail doesn't sound so bad.

JOHNNY: It isn't. Remember that.

Jail is a part of the life we lead, and it serves a
good purpose.

I need to change subjects and talk out loud
about a problem I have been having with my
bookie operation. We have too many
degenerate gamblers.

These gamblers lose and can't pay. The
economy is shit.

It's costing my operation a lot of money.

My bookies and I are getting too good at
manipulating gamblers to bet more than they
can afford.

No matter what walk of life they come from, we
understand how gamblers think.

We know that when gamblers bet, they think
they can always get back what they lost. When
gamblers win, there is no better high for them.

They chase that high. I have the same problem.

The secret is to encourage gamblers to bet more times per week, even on the same day, and bet on more sports.

If a gambler bets on a NFL game, then we convince them to bet on a basketball or hockey game.

The cardinal rule is the more a gambler bets, the more they lose, and the more we get in the end.

CARLO: How would a bookie go about manipulating a gambler to bet more?

JOHNNY: It's easy. I will be the bookie.

I start the conversation with the gambler as follows, "Hey, you see the game last night with the Knicks?"

The gambler goes, "Yeah, tough loss. I lost $200."

I empathize with him exhaling a heavy breath, "I lost $200 on that game also. I'll get it back tonight with the Rangers."

Immediately, he is hooked when he inquires, "Who are the Rangers playing? What is the spread?"

I confidently say, "Bruins by +2, it's a sure thing; I'm laying down $250."

He throws up a roadblock when he feebly sighs, "I'm tapped, and I can't afford anything right now. This week has been rough.

On Sunday, I lost $400 on the Giants and Cowboys. I'm in the hole for $1,100 so far this month."

I paint myself as on his side when I answer him with, "How about I give you $200 of your losses back to bet tonight?"

He leans forward and excitedly answers, "You would do that for me?"

I know I got him dangling from my hook, "Sure, I hate to see one of my guys lose, you're due for a win, let me try to help you get it back."

I'm his hero when he replies, "Wow, thanks."

Fast forward to four weeks later. I have a new conversation with my gambler. I tell him worriedly, "Hey, my boss is calling me asking to get caught up on everybody. Sorry I have to ask for this, but I need you to pay me what you owe."

He asks uncomfortably, "How much am I in the hole, $8,000?"

I reply, "$7,200, with what you won last night. Good job betting against the Patriots."

He delivers another roadblock, "My wife watches our accounts like a hawk and is going to freak out if I pull $7,200 out at one time."

Again, I am his hero when I ask him, "How about you pay me $800 a week until you are caught up?"

He replies, "You will do that for me? Thanks so much."

Then, there is a pause while he thinks, and he asks another question, "Can I get the Knicks tonight by +4 for $300?"

How many times have I seen this conversation play out? More than I can count.

Credit doesn't just work for the big banks; it works for us in gambling too. The good bookies know and practice this.

The great bookies are experts at it.

They know how much credit to give, when to give it, when to raise it, when to lower it, and when to collect on it. It is always easier to make money with a pen, than a gun.

CARLO: Makes sense. When a degenerate gambler can't pay, what happens?

JOHNNY: Depends. The old approach was one bookie would tell another bookie, "That guy owes you a lot of money. He is making you look like a schmuck. You are soft; no one will respect that they have to pay you. Why don't you send some guys over to take care of them and get your money? They only want 20%. They can break the guy's legs."

You know what happens if the bookie sends guys to collect?

The gambler gets scared, and fears for his life. Then, the gambler tells his wife.

She gets hysterical and calls the FBI. It's no good. We don't need that.

This may surprise you, but I try to avoid violence.

I have never been violent unless I have to be.

I always gained more through being nice to people. It is better to work with the gamblers who are in debt.

I tell my bookies to put them on a payment plan, get something out of them, whatever they can afford. Even if it's $50 or $100 per week, at least it's something.

Going forward, I want to avoid this whole collection problem entirely by developing a high-class gambling business for well-off people like doctors, lawyers and bankers. These gamblers can pay their debts.

I first thought, "What doctor, lawyer or banker would gamble with my bookies? My bookies are low-class and don't have access."

But then I asked myself a simple question, "What do doctors, lawyers and bankers do in their leisure time?"

One thing they do is golf, and when they golf, there is a lot of time on the course to talk about sports and place bets.

Can I send my bookies to the country clubs?

Who am I kidding?

No country club would let my bookies near it.

But then I had an idea, "What about sending a young caddy from the neighborhood over to one of these country clubs?"

CARLO: I could caddy for them.

JOHNNY: Right. You have been taking bets over the phone at the bar for the last couple weeks.

You have been learning how the gambling operation works.

For the bets, you write down the name, dollar amount, and teams they want.

Sometimes the caller asks your opinion on teams.

By the spring, you'll be an expert at it.

A few years from now, you'll be old enough to golf and make friends with these respectable guys.

You could run the whole high-class gambling business.

I know the guy who does the golf reservations for tee times. He can give you tips on doctor and lawyer groups.

Imagine when you learn how to golf.

My friend could call you when a group of doctors or lawyers need another guy to fill a tee time.

The call could go like this, "I got a 9:30 tomorrow morning with two lawyers, you want to join them?"

Then, the next day, you start out with a serious game for a few holes, then you start talking about sports with them.

You could say, "You see the game last night? Can you believe so and so did so and so?" That would get them going.

Pretty soon, you are golfing regularly with them and they are placing bets with you.

Your whole client list could be legitimate guys who are doctors, lawyers, bankers, wall street gurus, and professionals.

CARLO: I look forward to the opportunity. Thank you for thinking of it for me.

JOHNNY: No problem. You like jokes?

CARLO: Yeah, I hear from guys at the bar that you like to play practical jokes.

JOHNNY: I believe having a sense of humor is important.

One of my favorite jokes is to put a small amount of real gun powder in the cigarette ashtrays on the tables and bar.

The gun powder is grey like the cigarette ashes.

You have to look real hard to notice the difference.

No one ever does.

When a guy taps the ashes off his cigarette into the ashtray, and the tip of the cigarette is close enough to the gun powder to ignite it, there is a bright flash with a loud popping sound.

This is followed by a big puff of smoke.

It scares the living daylights out of those near it who scream obscenities while they check themselves for burns or wounds, which they never find.

Everyone else around them gets a good laugh out of it.

One time I took the joke a little too far and put too much gun powder in one of the ashtrays.

Suddenly, there was a small explosion with a bright yellow flash at least five feet high shaking the floor and seats in the bar and generating a ton of smoke.

A couple guys were covered with black soot from the smoke, nothing serious though.

CARLO: What a sight.

JOHNNY: The funniest part was the guy's hair, which stood straight up like a cartoon character.

He pulled out his pistol, waved it wildly above his head, and yelled, "I'm going to kill whoever did this, but then he found out it was you and quieted down."

JOHNNY: Due to the gun powder joke, some of the guys drive me nuts by flicking their ashes on the floor and making a mess.

I'll tell you a story about a good friend of mine who used to work with me up until a couple years ago.

He was a retired U.S. Navy Seal. He was an American hero who served our country for 20 years.

He retired to Miami about ten years ago where he met a beautiful blond, buxom girl.

He took his savings to buy a boat to spend his days exploring the Caribbean with his girl.

They left in the morning with a group of 100 boats to enjoy the water and sunshine all day.

This group all came back at about the same time every night before sunset.

At night, my friend made glorious love to his girl.

Most men would be envious of such a life, right? Not my friend. He quickly became bored.

He yearned for the action he had from his days in the Navy.

Even though he had looked forward to retirement for most of his life, he didn't quite realize what retirement would mean when he finally arrived there.

He became depressed. He wanted to feel alive again.

He needed something to challenge him and awaken his senses.

One afternoon, he was with his woman in the Bahamas having a drink at a seaside bar where he docked his boat.

He met one of my guys down there who was looking for help smuggling cocaine from the Bahamas to Miami.

My Navy friend heard stories about how dangerous and risky it was to drive a boat loaded with drugs in the waters off the Florida coastline past patrol boats from the DEA, the U.S. Coast Guard, and County Sheriffs.

Besides the patrol boats, flying high above the waters were DEA planes looking for anything suspicious below.

He thought this sounded a lot like his Navy experience.

He decided to add some excitement back into his life.

I hired him.

He described how the first load he did was better than any adrenaline high he experienced as a Navy Seal.

He felt alive again.

His life had a purpose.

He looked forward to the next time he could experience the same high.

He kept doing bigger and bigger loads to increase the danger and enhance the adrenaline rush he felt.

He did this for years successfully. He was happy.

CARLO: What was his secret to getting past all the cops patrolling the water and the air?

Did he have a fast cigarette boat that could outrun anything on the water?

JOHNNY: No, the DEA planes spot and encircle speed boats quickly.

What did he do? Let me answer that for you.

He hid in plain sight.

In the morning, he would leave with the same set of retired folks driving their boats into the open water.

Then, he went to a secluded drug loading point in the Bahamas.

At sunset, on the drive back among the large group of other boats, he had his beautiful girlfriend dressed in a tiny bikini jiggle her big tits as she waved at the cops in the patrol boats.

My Navy friend sat at the back of the boat and made a friendly hello gesture to the cops by raising his beer bottle.

The cops waved back with smiles.

My friend made a fortune.

He earned $2,000 for each kilo of cocaine he moved from the Bahamas to Miami.

I paid $10,000 in the Bahamas for each kilo.

Once in the U.S., a kilo was worth $35,000.

My Navy guy supplied not only me, but other guys across the country. He was one of the best.

Right before he got caught, he was doing single loads of 250 kilos.

That's $500,000 every trip.

CARLO: Wow, how did he get caught? A rat?

JOHNNY: How else? Yes, it was a rat.

The DEA gives money to low level guys like the ones who load the drugs on to the boats at the Bahamian docks.

These low-level guys aren't paid much.

My supplier gives us the loaders.

The rat described what my guy's boat looked like, what he looked like, everything, even the size of his girlfriend's tits.

On a random day, he was hit.

CARLO: What happened to the rat?

JOHNNY: Our supplier got a hold of him.

CARLO: How did the Navy guy handle being interrogated by the cops?

JOHNNY: After his arrest, he sat down with the DEA, Coast Guard and County Sheriff. They asked him how he got away with smuggling all those years.

They honestly didn't know.

He told them how simple his method was, and the cops hit the roof arguing about whose fault it was.

He said he felt like he could have walked out of the room and escaped!

He was a standup guy and didn't rat anybody out to reduce his sentence. The minimum mandatory sentence was 10 years for his case.

On the day of his sentencing, the judge said he never had such a decorated veteran stand before his bench. In the end, my friend's 20 years of Navy service counted for only 16 months off his ten-year sentence.

The judge said he couldn't believe the amount of greed the Navy guy displayed during his long smuggling career.

The judge didn't understand that it was never about the money.

He loved being in dangerous situations.

Time in jail wouldn't cure that.

Hey, you want to hear a joke?

Knock-knock.

CARLO: Who's there?

JOHNNY: Stan

CARLO: Stan Who?

JOHNNY: Stan back or I'll blow your fucking head off!

RIDE TO QUEENS

Johnny called and wanted me to drive his new Lincoln Town Car from Queens to a house in Clifton, NJ where he was wrapping up a meeting.

This was my first introduction to some of the things the Salerno family did and the type of people with whom Johnny was connected.

Johnny loved to laugh and spoke a hundred miles an hour as he jumped from topic to topic.

January 8, 2010

CARLO: Do you mind if I ask how your meeting went?

JOHNNY: (laughs) Yeah. The meeting was with my associate named "Schnaze." We call him that because of his big russet potato nose. He brought his partner, the slippery Irishman; we call him "Lucky Charms."

Both of these guys are pirates. They are small-time bookies, they deal drugs, steal construction equipment, run construction jobs, and own an excavation business.

Any money I earn with these two guys; I can't allow any of it to touch their hands.

The money can only go one way, from me to them.

They can't help themselves.

Schnaze gets contracts to tear down and demolish houses, and then haul the rubbish away.

What he enjoys most is before he starts work on a house; he goes inside and tries to salvage anything left abandoned by the previous occupants.

He says, "Look at this speaker, nothing wrong with it, it's good," as a mouse ran out the back before he loaded it on his semi-trailer truck.

Schnaze doesn't own anything new. Everything he owns is other people's junk.

Schnaze doesn't bathe and could be the centerfold spread for filth magazine.

His crooked yellow teeth, foul breath, and dirty neck don't help his slovenly appearance either.

He looks like he just came out from living under a bridge for the last five months, but, in his defense, he does own a house.

It is a moldy, teardown house that should be condemned with a dirt floor kitchen, but it is still a house.

Frankly, jail is the cleanest place Schnaze ever lived.

Nobody can walk barefoot in Schnaze's house without risking a foot infection or worse.

In the basement, his cat feasts off the mice and trash.

Schnaze has a problem with always dripping sweat, and he compounds this by never wearing a shirt.

He walks around his backyard wearing a nipple ring and wrinkled, saggy jeans without a belt.

A garbage dump is cleaner than his backyard. It is full of crap including: refrigerators dumped, abandoned cars missing wheels and doors, eight broken, rusted riding lawnmowers surrounded by seven-foot-high uncut grass, windows from a house piled up, and Christmas decorations.

There is a built-in pool that was dark green and looked like a swamp.

Vagabonds, borders and old truckers live in Schnaze's house so he can collect rent from them.

Those low-lifers lounge around the kitchen table all day or sit on the deck outside smoking cigarettes.

They barbeque meat on a cheap, beat up $69 gas grill that looks like it has been thrown out 10 different times by as many different owners before it was garbage-picked by Schnaze.

Next to the grill is a 30-gallon empty grease drum filled with cigarette butts.

Schnaze's car is a 1995 white, rusted Pontiac Bonneville with 250,000 miles.

Loaded inside the car is a dumpster's worth of old McDonald's bags and loose garbage.

He hides the drugs he sells under the garbage.

No cop ever checks for drugs inside such a mess for fear of being bitten by a small animal if he did.

Next to the Bonneville, Schnaze keeps his fleet of old semi-trailer trucks held together with duct tape and super glue.

One positive thing I can say about Schnaze is he is a great father. He would do anything for his son. He spoils the 10-year-old rotten.

The kid is a roly-poly. His whole diet is junk food, soda pop, and McDonald's French fries. Schnaze can be guilty of treating Giovanni like a Doberman though when he yells, "Basta Giovanni!" This means in Italian, "Stop it Giovanni! I've had it up to here with you!"

Giovanni's mother isn't his current woman. Years ago, Schnaze knocked up the kid's mother after getting her hooked on heroin and weed.

He got custody of the kid when the kid's mother went to jail for drugs.

Honestly, it is hard for me to imagine Schnaze having sex with any woman.

He used to tell me how he would be on his waterbed rolling around with his woman on the rubberized surface with no sheets and a gallon of vegetable oil.

The thought of it disgusts me.

Schnaze's current woman was there at the beginning of the meeting. I hadn't met her before today.

Initially, I thought she was Greek due to her mustache.

She wore what looked like a pool table covering with a hole cut in the top as a dress.

Her nails were chewed up.

She's the type of woman who greets you with "Eat Shit", instead of "Good morning" or "Hello."

What a blown out, shark bait, miserable, big mouth.

She is a nurse for hospice patients. Her hustle is she steals their oxycodone pills and replaces them with aspirin.

She divides the pills, half for her and Schnaze, and the other half she sells for $50 a pill.

She is bossy and a vegan. She's a real jerk about being a vegan.

I heard last week her and Schnaze went out to dinner and she discovered the restaurant chef grilled her vegetables in the same place where he grilled meat.

She blew a gasket at the chef, and the manager asked them to leave the restaurant.

I'll tell you a little about the man we call Lucky Charms.

Lucky's first word to any woman he meets is "Oy", followed by a blank stare where he gawks at their tits for fifteen seconds trying to imagine his own Penthouse forum sex fantasy.

Lucky wears a dirty toupee.

He bragged recently about how the cops recently thought he had millions of dollars hidden in a large safe in his basement.

He went on to say that when the cops raided his place, they called a locksmith to blow the safe open.

Guess what was inside?

As a joke, Lucky put two of his toupees in there. The cops were furious and left.

Today, when I arrived at the house Lucky and Schnaze were in a conversation.

Lucky said, "If I ever go to jail, I want to bring my toupees with me".

Schnaze countered, "I don't think they allow you to bring toupees with you to jail. Besides, why do you care about what you look like in jail?"

Lucky retorted, "In case people come to visit me, I want to look my best."

Lucky sat at the kitchen table next to a phone that constantly rang where he took bets on sport games, "+4 Giants, -6 Jets, Knicks by +2, Rutgers by +8."

He told me about the breakfast place where he goes every morning to conduct the payoffs and pickups for his bookie operation.

He claims, "You wouldn't believe the amount of senior citizens who gamble!"

He chose the place because he gets a free senior citizen cup of coffee and he steals sugar to fill a glass jar at home in his kitchen.

Lucky is cheap.

He takes piles of napkins and anything else he can snatch.

Lucky complained about his wife he just divorced, who he had recently married after living with her for 10 years and raising her two children.

After all the years they lived together, Lucky wanted to reward her loyalty by marrying her even though he hadn't been loyal.

He cheated on her the entire time.

After their wedding, Lucky came to find out she wasn't loyal either.

She had been cheating on him with a German guy named, "Ham."

He divorced her.

Last week, Schnaze told me how he bet $1,000 on each of five different NFL football games.

Before he placed the bets, he called Lucky to recommend five winners.

All five teams Lucky picked lost.

Schnaze yelled, "It's harder to pick five losers than it is to pick one winner!"

Shortly after, Schnaze got Lucky back by sticking him with a huge dinner bill in Atlantic City at one of those restaurants that has a gift shop which sells souvenirs.

It turns out Schnaze excused himself early from the dinner, went to the restaurant gift shop, and charged four bags of stuff including sweatshirts, coffee mugs, keychains, and T-shirts to Lucky's table.

Lucky said when he received the bill, he yelled at the waitress, "This is large enough for a football team! I'm not paying for this! I'm only paying for my portion!"

Lucky is probably most well-known for his nickname, the "King of Garbage," from his excavation business he owns in collusion with Schnaze.

Lucky spends many of his days moving contaminated soil and garbage from one place to another.

Recently, a developer in Manhattan had a site for a large building that was prepared to start construction. In the middle of the night, Lucky dumped a big pile of contaminated soil on the developer's site that he picked up from a gas station which had a tank leak underground.

The soil smelled like gas and shit.

The next morning, Schnaze, who was the site construction manager, and, of course, Schnaze was in on the scam called the developer nervously saying, "Oh boy, do we have a problem, boss.

Somebody dumped a real mess on our job site.

The site inspectors from the EPA and OSHA are due to arrive later today.

They could potentially declare this a hazardous waste site and delay construction.

What do you want me to do?"

The developer feverishly asked, "Can you find someone to haul it away ASAP?"

Schnaze slyly offered, "It will be expensive, but I can get a hold of a friend of mine."

Schnaze summoned Lucky to return to the same site to pick up the same soil he dumped six hours ago.

Lucky billed the developer for $900 a truck load for 10 trips that totaled $9,000, which was the same total he billed the gas station!

Then, Lucky moved the same soil once more to a large mansion in Rumson where he had a contract to fill a large empty pool in the back yard that the wealthy homeowner no longer wanted.

Lucky got paid three times for moving the same soil from the gas station, to the Manhattan developer's site, and finally to the Jersey mansion owner.

Beautiful, isn't it?

Here's another, even better story.

Every summer Lucky goes into empty, abandoned lots in Newark, puts up a fence, and dumps garbage.

The piles get up to 100 feet high.

The wind blows the wrong way and entire neighborhoods smell the fermenting shit.

The neighborhood calls the city officials yelling, "We can't take it anymore! Look at the mountain of garbage in our city!"

Guess who wins the contract from the mayor to remove the garbage?

The same guy who put it there.

Lucky is a multimillionaire, but he pisses his money away every chance he gets.

Lucky irritates me every now and then.

He calls the red sauce for pasta "gravy." Irish kids didn't grow up eating pasta and red sauce. They ate it when they went over to their Italian friends' houses for dinner. They liked it so much the Irish kids would go home to their Irish mothers and tell them about the "gravy" their friends' mothers poured over the pasta.

To this day, we still have a big argument over whether to call it "sauce" or "gravy".

I went to my old, Italian uncle to help clear this up and he said the true Italian name is "zugo" which means "sauce."

This is what an asshole Lucky Charms is. He goes to an Irish food market in Queens and finds a jar with the label marked "Italian Gravy."

He shoves the jar in my face and says, "See? Fuck you!"

I said, "What do you know about being Italian? You ever hear of Louie Prima?"

Lucky said no.

I told him, "Louis Prima is the Italian Elvis."

This is when Schnaze jumped in the conversation, pointed one finger to the sky and declared, "I'm Italian, and I never heard of Louie Prima!"

I turned red in the face, "You're Italian, and you never heard of Louie Prima? You're a fucking low class Italian, a hillbilly Italian.

What about Mario Lanza, you ever hear of him?"

"No," Schnaze weakly replied.

"You just proved my point!" I exclaimed.

Then, Lucky and Schnaze started arguing about why there are no roller rinks in their neighborhood anymore.

They came to the conclusion that people today are too fat, and if they fell down, they could never get up.

They talked about how today a 400-pound man is what a 200-pound man was thirty years ago.

Nonsense, complete nonsense.

Ironically, they both earn individually over $80,000 in cash a month, but they are always broke.

They ask to borrow money from me.

I scold them, "Where did all the money go?"

They shrug it off, "We went out for ribs with our friends."

I call their bluff, "Bullshit, $80,000 for ribs?

I know you both go to Atlantic City every weekend to play the $100 pull slot machines and sit at the poker tables."

Schnaze and Lucky are both degenerate gamblers and it gets them into real trouble even though Lucky is a bookie himself.

One time, they burned another family's bookie with $250,000 in outstanding gambling debts.

The bookie nearly had a heart attack over it until he went to a Salerno boss to ask for permission to dynamite Schnaze's house.

I had to get involved to calm everyone down.

To make things right, and get the bookie paid, Schnaze and Lucky went on a two-man crime wave in the tri-state area hitting construction sites and stealing equipment over last Labor Day weekend.

They stole construction equipment like a hammer used to break a bridge, an excavator with a five-yard bucket, a front-end loader, a compactor over here, a steamroller over there. It adds up to big money.

CARLO: I never heard of this equipment. How much is it worth?

JOHNNY: The steamroller? A buck thirty-five. The hammer? A buck twenty-five. Frontend loader? Two-fifty.

CARLO: $135? $125? $250? That's it? Sound like a waste of time to me.

JOHNNY: Pay attention. It's big money like I said. It's $135,000 for the bridge hammer, $125,000 for the steamroller, and $250,000 for the loader.

CARLO: How do they steal such big equipment? What did they do with the equipment once they have it?

JOHNNY: Hah! Good questions. Well, they had lots of options. Being the snake that he is, Schnaze paid $2,000 to a guy at one of the construction sites to load a $135,000 hammer into his semi-trailer early in the morning.

For the $250,000 front end loader that Lucky recently boosted in Jersey City, he drove it to a mall parking lot in Poughkeepsie where I had a $500,000 snow removal contract for the winter.

I planned to burn the machine out on the job all winter and part it out at the end when spring comes.

CARLO: What do you mean by the term "part it out"?

JOHNNY: People wonder why their insurance rates are so high. They can thank Schnaze and Lucky Charms.

There's a huge business in truck dismemberment: engines, rear ends, bumpers, hoods, or anything.

It's all money and in demand.

Schnaze and Lucky buy junk trucks all the time, especially the R-models from the sixties to the eighties.

Lucky stole a $40,000 brand new, beautiful wrecking semi-trailer.

Then, he had his mechanic reassemble it on a 1960 trailer where he had a title in his name.

He went around and told everyone his mechanic built the trailer custom for him.

Back to Schnaze and Lucky's gambling, I have a funny story about how they antagonize a certain type of low-level bookie, usually located in Manhattan.

This type of bookie lies to his gamblers and claims he is connected to one of the crime families, but he isn't.

When a bookie says he is connected to a family, gamblers think they need to pay their debts or risk getting their legs broken.

This gives the bookie clout over his gamblers.

The problem is any young kid can get into the bookie business by going around and claiming he is part of a family.

There are new bookies like this sprouting up all the time.

My bookies and bookies from other families compete with these scumbags.

They cut into our profits.

As a hobby, Schnaze and Lucky help me out by circling Manhattan looking for these fraudulent bookies.

Schnaze and Lucky gamble so much that they know all the legitimate bookies from the families and can spot a fake.

When they find one, Schnaze and Lucky lie to the fake bookie and say they represent a really big spender.

The bookie is ecstatic that he has a new customer.

The bookie asks for a cash deposit of $5,000 to begin accepting their bets.

Schnaze and Lucky initially place a few bets to build some trust.

Then, after a few months, they place more bets.

They collect if they win, and don't pay if they lose.

Eventually, they rack up a huge debt.

The bookie reaches his breaking point when he tells Schnaze and Lucky he can't accept their bets anymore.

The bookie asks for his money.

Schnaze and Lucky tell the bookie, "We just want to let you know that the big spender we represent is Johnny Toracio from 101st Avenue."

When the bookie hears my name, he nearly soils himself.

He forgives the debt and parts ways.

If the bookie knows any other fraudulent bookies, he warns them, "What was I thinking taking a bet from these guys?! They don't pay! Avoid taking any bets from them!"

CARLO: Funny story.

JOHNNY: I'll tell you about a weekend down in Atlantic City I spent with Schnaze and Lucky a few weeks ago.

Boy, did I regret it!

The rooms they chose were garbage.

You can call the rooms the Presidential Suite for $29 a night with 100-year-old carpet, two-inch cigar burns in each arm of the sofa chair, every tile in the bathroom cracked, couches from the 1970's, a tiny microwave, and a two-jet hot tub.

They tried to get me to stay in an adjacent room and I went ballistic.

I called it the "Schlep-Rock" Suite.

They liked the hotel because it had an entryway with an Elvis statue, but the statue was missing Elvis' nose and one of his hands.

The hotel pool was green with an old, Swedish, giant dude in a translucent speedo bouncing around in the water.

He had no shame at all - the audacity of him.

I wanted to throw up.

Then, those two morons took me to their favorite strip club, a real dive, off the Atlantic City boardwalk where a 200-pound stripper stuck her tongue in my ear.

I was so grossed out I had to wash my ear with a shot of vodka before I left.

The stripper had pimpled tits and an unshaved jungle below.

She was complete trash, the worst.

To show Schnaze and Lucky how to do a gambling trip right, I took them last week to Vegas with me.

I rented one of those large suites at the Bellagio where we could all stay.

The suite had multiple bedrooms, a large bar, 15-foot-high ceilings, a view of the strip, and its own bowling alley!

The first night we stayed there, I left the suite early without them and went to a strip club named Gentleman Jacks, where I know the guys who run the place.

I brought 30 ecstasy pills with me. I popped a few, and I was having a great time.

All of the women at the club were gorgeous, and one started talking to me.

We hit it off.

I offered her a couple pills.

She took them and began dancing wildly.

Then, she called her friend over, and I gave her a couple pills.

It was getting late. I asked if they both wanted to keep partying with me.

She gave me an address of a club to meet her after her shift.

I assumed this was her bullshit way of getting rid of me.

Before I left, she asked for 6 more pills and I gave them to her.

I went to the address of the club they gave me on the slight chance they would come. Low and behold, the two girls did.

I asked them if they wanted to come back to my suite. They agreed.

I was thinking, "Can this really be happening? I must be dreaming."

When we arrived at the Bellagio, I left the girls in the lobby while I ran up to check the suite. Before I took the girls up there, I wanted to make sure Schnaze and Lucky were gone. The suite was empty.

I guessed Schnaze and Lucky were at the poker tables for an all-nighter.

The suite was mine for the two girls.

We had a threesome.

We had so much fun that the girls missed their 4am flight to Los Angeles.

Then, right before we finished, Schnaze and Lucky banged on the door.

Lucky yelled from the hallway, "Johnny, are you in there? Let us in."

Schnaze and Lucky couldn't get in the room with their keys because I locked and chained the door behind me when the girls and I originally went into the suite.

I responded from behind the door, "I got girls in here."

Lucky yelled, "You got girls in there?"

Lucky didn't understand that this meant I wanted him to leave.

He thought I meant I had extra girls for him and Schnaze.

I clarify to him, "The girls are for me and get out of here."

Lucky responded, "What?"

Now I was pissed. I undid the chain and opened the door.

Lucky charged past me.

Before I could tackle him, he dropped his pants and drawers to exclaim, "Who's going to ball me?!"

Lucky thought the girls were hookers.

The girls got scared, grabbed their clothes, and ran out the door.

I can't blame them.

I roared at Lucky, "I'm the boss! You don't go after my girls unless I give you permission, understood?

You ruined my fun!

The girls are gone!

You and Schnaze need to get out of here!"

Then, an hour later the girls left me urgent voicemails that they still wanted to party despite Lucky's vulgar behavior, but I didn't get the messages until the next morning after I woke up.

By that time, the girls had already caught their flight to LA.

CARLO: Did you ever talk to the girls again?

JOHNNY: Yeah, I told them to give me a call if they were ever in New York. A month later, they asked me to pick them up at LaGuardia airport.

Then, one shocked me when she said, "It is $1,000 to party with me."

I told her, "You are in New York now. This is my city.

I don't pay for anything.

You want to go out and have a good time, then great. If not, forget it."

She passed on my offer. I was dumbfounded.

Lucky was right. They were hookers!

Usually, I don't pick up hookers without knowing it. And when I do, I like groups of hookers because I have a better time.

This reminds me of a hooker story.

The other night I was in one of those two-story motels with an outdoor hallway and the rooms are all in a row each with a door and a front window.

I had four hookers.

We needed more ecstasy pills to keep the party flying high.

It was around 3:30am when I called Lucky to deliver it, and I asked him to knock on my room's window when he arrived.

90 minutes went by and I wondered where Lucky was.

As I chased the naked women around the room, I glanced at the window, and I could see Lucky's eyes peeking through a slight opening in the drapes.

What a pervert!

Instead of charging in and trying to be part of the fun like he did in Vegas, Lucky thought he would watch.

I locked eyes with him, and he saw my rage.

He left the pills at the door and ran away.

I had a hell of a time that night because nobody heard from me for a week!

Where were we?

CARLO: You were telling me about the jobs Schnaze and Lucky do.

JOHNNY: Yeah. Both Lucky and Schnaze are connected to several towns in Jersey where they are able to bill the town halls for bogus jobs like repairing a broken water main where there is no water main.

Then, they split the money with the mayor or council member, and make off like bandits.

Schnaze and Lucky are fast too.

If I need anything like a bobcat at a construction site, they'll throw one in one of their trucks and have it at my job that day.

They're great.

CARLO: Wouldn't they go to jail for doing that?

JOHNNY: Trust me. Everybody goes to jail eventually, even honest people.

During my last jail bid, one of the guys down the hall was an accountant who did the books for a bunch of crooked companies that had millions of dollars in fake, ghost inventories.

CARLO: What is a ghost inventory?

JOHNNY: Picture a warehouse with boxes stacked from floor to ceiling. The boxes are stacked 30 deep and the boxes in the front are full of merchandise.

The boxes in back are all empty.

If you own a company and count all the boxes as full of inventory even though most are empty, this is worth big bucks in your pocket and is what is called a ghost inventory.

From the accountant's point of view, he is the guy who has to sign off on the inventories.

He vouches for the books, but there is an obvious flaw in this system.

What is the accountant going to do?

Should he go to these warehouses and inspect every box to make sure they are full of product?

The accountant is busy. He has too many other clients with too many other warehouses.

Listen to this. Next, the feds came knocking on the door of the crooked companies asking questions.

Push came to shove, and the crooked owners try to save their own asses.

They blamed the accountant.

They convinced the prosecutor the accountant was the person who created the fake inventories!

And the feds believed it!

During the accountant's trial, the prosecutor stood outside the courthouse, waved his finger in the air as he told the media, "the accountant mastermind behind it all deserves to be put away for the maximum penalty under the law!"

The accountant was found guilty and the judge threw him in jail for five years.

Can you believe it? Five years! The whole notion is absurd.

If anything, the accountant was guilty of being gullible because he trusted the crooked owners.

It happens all the time.

Jail is full of guys like my accountant friend.

The government calls it the Department of Justice, but I call it the Department of Injustice!

The accountant really was clueless about how his life took such a dramatic turn sideways.

I can tell when someone is lying, and this guy wasn't.

When I talked to him in jail, he kept asking me, "Why am I here? Why did they put me here?"

I felt bad for him. Another guy down the hall from me was a lawyer.

He pissed off prosecutors for years because he won all of his Wall Street cases involving insider trading and securities fraud.

One prosecutor nailed the lawyer with a bogus IRS tax evasion case, and the judge gave him three years in jail.

It's a brutal world out there.

When the lawyer was sent to jail, he was an old man at 70 years old, but he tried to make the best out of the situation.

He could mix a hell of a drink for us.

CARLO: You drank alcohol in jail?

JOHNNY: What else are we going to do?

This lawyer could mix a drink that would knock an elephant on its ass.

After the third drink, you felt like someone dropped a bowling ball on your head from the 10th floor of a building.

Oh yeah, the drinks would be flowing, and the joints would be glowing to pass the time.

Yeah, we smoked weed in jail too.

I empathize with the guards.

They have to try catch us when we do all this stuff.

They place their own lives in danger too.

There are some real psychopaths in jail. Guys who have a screw loose. You can call them asocial, which means they don't like interacting with or talking to other people. They are dangerous to the guards and the other inmates.

I remember a story about a guard who confiscated the headphones of a psychopath because one of the wires on the headphones had been repaired with electrical tape.

Inmates aren't allowed to have repaired items like this.

The problem for the guard with confiscating the headphones is guys in jail don't have much property and many guys don't have income coming in from the outside to replace confiscated property.

The next day the psychopath hid behind a door in his cell.

When the guard peeked in, he got stabbed with a three-inch shank 50 times in a matter of seconds.

One inch of blood covered the floor.

Confiscate a psychopath's property in jail and anything can happen.

I am a normal guy. I can make sense of things. I am not a psychopath. Sometimes, I can't believe I get put with those animals when I get jammed up on a case and get a sentence.

For normal people like me, I try to make sure I have a good lawyer to keep me away from jail. I don't belong there.

CARLO: Who is the lawyer you use?

JOHNNY: My lawyer is a funny guy.

He says, "You know when I am called? I'm called when somebody has been in an accident. Nobody calls me before the accident because no one ever expects to be in an accident.

They call me after the accident, and they need someone to come in, assess the damage, clean up the mess, and get everyone back to the regular lives again with minimal disruption!"

For my last case, he said, "You are looking at 15+ years. This is one hell of an accident!

I have a lot of cleaning up to do. I am an expert at getting my clients what they want, even when they don't deserve it. I can tell you one thing.

The only time I look down on a man is when I am extending my hand to help him up.

What I mean by saying this is I am here for you and I am working on some things in your plea bargain negotiations that are helpful to you."

Lawyers are all just like us, maybe even better.

He told me about his scheme, "I have several friends who are senior partners at various big private practice law firms around town and they are always in search of hiring talented lawyers to help with their growing business."

I asked him, "How does this apply to me?"

He laughed, "I'm glad you asked. It just so happens at this very moment the three key opposing lawyers who are in charge of prosecuting you on behalf of the U.S. government, the U.S. Attorney, the Assistant U.S. Attorney and the Head of the Organized Crime Unit, are all being heavily recruited by those big law firms I just described."

He continued, "Do you mind if I use a sports analogy to explain this strategy? Please forgive me for using a sports analogy because this game we play is serious and affects the rest of your life!

Do you like baseball?

Let's just say I am on your team, the home team.

We are the good guys who the crowd cheers for and hopes wins.

The government is the opposing team.

They are the bad guys.

The crowd boos at them and hopes they lose.

Let me ask you, what is the goal of everyone in the minor leagues?

To get into the major leagues so they can live the good life, and sign that multi-year, big contract.

They want to be successful.

Now, if I can put major league contracts into the hands of the entire opposing team just before their last game in the minor leagues, what do you think will happen during their last game?

They won't give a shit.

Do you think your team's chances of winning against this opposing team during their last game increased or decreased?"

I told him, "My team is a sure thing to win."

He laughed again, "Guess what, your case is their last game! You'll be back home with your family in no time. The only place success comes before work is in the dictionary!"

Let me change subjects.

I have a few things to cover with you.

Now that you're with me, in some ways you represent me.

You know what that means?

CARLO: Yeah, I need to always show respect toward others.

Be a gentleman.

Respect is how I treat people and how I act.

Common courtesies mean a lot like "please, thank you, excuse me, I beg your pardon."

JOHNNY: Yeah, and dress sharp by wearing a nice shirt, tie, tailored suit, and shoes.

The shoes are important. They need to be Italian-made, shined, and black leather.

Tuck the shoelaces inside the shoe like this.

And cufflinks for the white dress shirt need to be real gold, with your initials like this.

And see this lighter? Always a custom lighter like this with your initials, the larger the flame, the better.

You have a lot to learn. I am not going to do all the teaching. Others will help.

I am not a treacherous guy. I am a gentleman. I say hello to people, I ask people I know how their families are, and I wish people well during the holidays.

You can begin working with the others soon enough. There are some new retail places that need to fall in line. You can be a part of that.

These places haven't learned the lesson.

The lesson is you open a store in our neighborhood; you have to pay the tax.

No matter who you are, everybody pays the tax, the Salerno family tax.

CARLO: Got it.

JOHNNY: Did you hear the story about how I got the club manager in line from Manhattan the other night when he disrespected Lucky?

Lucky had a girlfriend who wanted to quit as a bartender in a joint that was connected to another family. She asked him to come with her when she told the manager she wanted to quit. When she tried to quit, the manager ordered her, "You ain't going anywhere. Get back behind the bar."

Lucky stood up for the girl and told the manager, "She's done working there, and that's it."

The manager yelled at Lucky, "Who the hell are you? Get out of here before I put a gun in your face."

Lucky replied, "Look, you don't know who I am, and I don't know who you are. How about we handle this through our people? I'll go to my boss, and you can go to your boss. This will all get sorted out. I know Johnny from 101st avenue."

The manager didn't believe Lucky knew me, and he attempted to call Lucky's bluff by saying, "I don't care who you know, and I don't care about Johnny! I am not afraid of Johnny."

Lucky told the manager, "Ok, no problem, I am going to leave."

Lucky went straight to me. When I heard what happened, I wanted to see the manager.

When we arrived, I walked in slowly wearing a long black overcoat.

The manager shrieked, "Look, I had no idea! I thought your friend was bullshitting me! I am sorry! Please, I don't want any problems! I meant no disrespect!"

In the back of the club, I saw stairs.

I pointed to them, and calmly told the manager, "We're going down to the basement."

When we got to the bottom of the stairs, I faced him and ordered, "Get down on your knees right now."

Then, I jammed my .357 revolver in his mouth and declared, "I don't care who owns this place.

I want $500 a week out of here.

Do you understand?"

CARLO: Nobody can shake a place down like you.

JOHNNY: Thanks. You ever hear of Omerta?

It's our code of silence.

There is nobility and honor in living by our code of silence.

Remember that only rats write books.

Don't believe a word of it. It's all lies.

The rats provide the only understanding that the general public has of our life in La Cosa Nostra.

The real wiseguy lives by Omerta and never talks about the life.

One time, a friend of mine wore a wire.

The day he wore it I knew something was wrong because he asked me questions about things, where I knew, he already knew the answer.

Also, his mannerisms were different.

When you know someone for so many years, you notice very small things, and you know what they think and say.

I thought in the back of my head, this isn't the guy I know. I clammed up.

He didn't trick me into confessing to anything, and since he was unsuccessful with me, he received a longer sentence in jail for not being able to save his own ass at the expense of others.

My uncle is the only member of my family who I have left as a parent figure.

I know that he loves me, but he rarely shows it. In fact, I can only remember one time when he expressed his true feeling toward me, and he did it when he was drunk.

My uncle comes from a different background than me, by that I mean he was a legitimate guy who worked in construction for his whole life.

The fact that he was able to express himself meant a lot to me.

It was shortly after I was sentenced eight years ago. He said he was proud of me that I took it like a man.

CARLO: What does that mean to take it like a man? That you accepted responsibility for your past actions?

JOHNNY: Not so much that. It had more to do with the fact that I wasn't a rat. Not being a rat is like wearing a badge of honor in our neighborhood. People stop me on the street. They give me praise and respect for not being a rat. It means I am a standup guy, a trustworthy guy.

I would never think to rat on others, but, if I did, what does it get me?

When you're a rat, it is a lifetime sentence.

You may go into the witness protection program. You have to move away from all of your family and friends.

Most importantly, you are looking over your shoulder for the rest of your life.

Me? The ordeal was over. I got to start a new life, a worry-free life.

I went back to my neighborhood, and I wrote my own ticket going forward.

CARLO: Makes sense. What is the selling point of being a rat?

JOHNNY: In a rat's defense, the rat sometimes has a legitimate beef with a boss. The beefs could be the rat may have always felt picked on by the boss, the rat could have felt the boss always gave him shitty jobs, or the rat may feel like he kicked money up to the boss for years without ever getting a "thank you" for all the hard work he did and the risking of his life he may have done.

Then, a federal case comes along where the boss' fate is in the rat's hands, and the rat turns on the boss over spite.

In another example, the rat may feel he has a beef with someone in the family. For example, on my case, the FBI played me tapes of my friend saying he was going to kill me and take over my business. But, in all seriousness, we always talked like that behind each other's backs. My friend was probably just breaking balls. Occasionally, it could be taken out of context.

It all goes back to the Rico act almost twenty years ago which started the decline of everything.

CARLO: Rico act?

JOHNNY: The Racketeering act. It means no evidence is needed anymore to convict a wiseguy. Only hearsay is needed, and it usually comes from a low-level guy who gets jammed up on a case. What happens next is the low-level guy gets threatened by the feds with 20 years to life in jail. The feds tell him, "You are going to protect the boss? Give us what we need, and you will walk out of here."

The low level guy strikes a deal to avoid that much time, and names a bunch of others who are higher up in the organization, including the boss.

What follows is the feds go visit the others named by the rat, and threaten a new case on each of them. This is when one is tempted to become the second rat. If he gives in to the temptation, then all of a sudden the boss is named by two different people, and the boss is done. All the feds need to throw the boss behind bars is two people naming him, and the boss gets charged with racketeering.

Remember, all of this occurred with hearsay. In federal cases, the conviction rate is over 97%. In states, it's over 50%. The feds hold all the power. If you get a fed case, then you plead it out, but you don't rat. Organizations these days have taken a major hit because of the Rico act.

CARLO: I have to get this straight. The boss gets locked up without any hard evidence because two criminals point their finger at him and say he's the boss?

JOHNNY: Yeah. It doesn't sound like the United States of America does it? The drug conspiracy laws are worse. Two dope fiends point at a drug dealer in court and say he sold them drugs for years. The prosecutor asks one dope fiend, "How much drugs did this man sell you over the past five years?"

The dope fiend answers, "at least five pounds of methamphetamines."

Boom, that's enough to put the dealer away for life. Federal judges hand out life sentences like they are candy.

CARLO: Ouch. How does La Cosa Nostra stay alive despite the Rico act or Drug Conspiracy laws?

JOHNNY: This organization has been around for over a 100 years.

Every time 10 guys go away to jail, there are another five are coming out of jail, and they don't care, they will go back to doing what they have always been doing.

In addition, there are another 5-10 coming up, who are young like you, and who are ready to take their place.

That is why we will last forever.

Let me put a situation before you.

A real wiseguy is in a court room and standing in front of a judge who is handing down the wiseguy's sentence for crimes he committed. The sentence is harsh. The wiseguy gets life in prison with no chance for probation.

My question to you is how should the wiseguy respond to the judge at this very moment?

CARLO: A real wiseguy takes it like a man and accepts his sentence with a smile, right?

JOHNNY: I like you kid. You will go far in this life with that attitude.

Now let me put one more situation before you.

If the same wiseguy's lawyer for the same case for some reason unknown to the wiseguy is able to get the criminal charges against him dropped, how should the wiseguy respond to the lawyer?

CARLO: I don't know. Should he thank him?

JOHNNY: You surprised me with your answer.

Yeah, he should thank him.

Make no mistake; a real wiseguy is fearless and ready to do the jail time for his crimes at any time.

Let me tell you something about the cops in our neighborhoods.

You notice the police car that just drove by us? Did you see the words, "to serve and protect," on the cop car's rear fender?

In our neighborhoods, the cops don't "serve and protect."

They "profit and neglect."

Every one of the cops you see around here works for the Salerno family.

Cops are like elephants in the circus.

Instead of gobbling up peanuts from our hands, the cops gobble up the cash we give them.

I'm going to give you a job as a runner.

A runner takes brown bags full of cash, and, at precise locations and times, he throws the bags into open windows of cop cars.

Let's say a cop car pulls up to a donut shop, cop gets out, goes into the shop, and leaves his passenger window open. You emerge from the alley, walk by the car, toss in a brown bag that falls to the passenger side floor inside the car. You keep walking down the street; cop walks out, gets into the car, and drives away. You see the cop opening the bag, and he is gobbling up the peanuts you gave him as he smiles.

When it comes to the FBI, no matter how hard they try, they can never truly think like a criminal. They are good guys. These two agents that hassle me all the time are named Agents Bridgeton and Matera. They have put away a lot of my friends.

They are good at what they do, and they have been doing it for quite a while, however, they are not great at what they do. They never can be.

Being a criminal is not in their DNA.

One problem the FBI always has is like in any organization, the more people involved, the greater likelihood for error.

When they are about to close in or are watching what I am doing, they leave little signs everywhere.

A car will drive by in the neighborhood with a driver who just doesn't look like he fits in or the driver is a little too alert observing people on the sidewalk. Or it might be a guy with sunglasses standing on a street corner in a sanitation crew uniform watching people.

A good criminal like me can spot these fakes from a mile away.

When the two agents from the FBI decided to raid my house a couple years ago, I was vacationing in Hawaii.

I stayed in Waikiki with a girl, and we had a great time.

One morning, I was in my room and I received a call from Agent Matera who I knew because he subpoenaed me a number of times.

The agent was a real gentleman throughout the process and I knew I could talk to him.

Agent Matera said, "Hey Johnny, we are at your house with some guys and we have more guys on their way to your hotel where you are staying, so please do not flee. We will find you."

I answered, "I'm not going anywhere. Where would I go?"

He told me, "We are going to enter your house and seize everything."

I asked him, "Whatever you do, please don't kick the door down at the house and trash the place. The key to the front door is with my neighbor next door. They will give it to you no problem. You can go through whatever you need at the house no problem. Will you let me turn myself in back there?"

He said, "Look Johnny, you have been gracious every time we have contacted you. Can you make it here by Monday morning to turn yourself in?"

I turned myself in just like I said I would.

CARLO: The FBI agent sounds like a decent guy. Do you mind if I change subjects and ask you a personal question about how you came to have only one arm? Was the other one shot off in an epic gun street battle?

JOHNNY: No, nothing of the sort. I don't mind talking about it with you. Not many people ask me about it. I lost most of my one arm when I was an 11-year-old kid.

I remember playing in the street in the summer with friends, and there was an open fire hydrant with water gushing out on the street.

I stood in front of it and the water knocked me backward.

One of my arms extended out into the oncoming traffic to break my fall.

A bus drove by and took off most of my left arm. See? I just have a small stump.

CARLO: How tragic. What was it like when you went back to school?

JOHNNY: At that age, kids are not nice and can be mean and hurtful.

The whole experience toughened me up.

Several bullies at my school saw my new handicap as a sign of weakness.

There was one bully who sat in front of me in class.

This jerkoff took a sadistic pleasure in what he did every day to me.

It took place before the school bell, at 10 minutes to 2pm.

The bully would turn around, give me an evil smile, put his hands together, and start cracking each of his knuckles as he threatened, "Get ready you little twerp, here comes another beating!"

Every day when this ritual began, I didn't have the guts to look the bully back in the eyes when he looked at me, so I looked down.

I was trying to hold back tears as I awaited my fate.

One day, my anger toward the bully built up to the point where it gave me the courage to let go of my fear.

I decided I wasn't going to get beat up anymore. On this day at 10 minutes to 2pm, the bully turned around to face me like he always did.

But I didn't look down.

I stared right back into the bully's eyes and gave him an evil smile first.

He hesitated for a moment.

Without thinking, I grabbed a pencil, raised it above my head, and stabbed it through his hand.

The bully cried out in pain and tears welled up in his eyes.

I liked this new feeling of power. It liberated me from an albatross of fear. But I wasn't done. I made a fist, aimed it at the edge of the bully's jaw with ferocious intensity, and knocked him out cold in his seat.

The rest of the class cheered as I let out a triumphant laugh and sat back in my chair.

The teacher looked over in horror and covered her mouth before yelling at me.

From that day forward, word quickly spread at the school and in the neighborhood, and no one ever picked on me again.

The school principal suspended me for a week and ordered my parents to have me evaluated by a psychiatrist before I was allowed to return.

The psychiatrist diagnosed me with ADHD, attention deficit, hyperactivity disorder, and prescribed me a drug at the time to help relax me called Ritalin.

I didn't take my Ritalin as prescribed. Instead, I smashed up the pills several at a time and sniffed them to get high.

That was the beginning of my experimentation with every possible drug or illegal substance I could find, and it still plagues me to this day.

I never made it to high school. I saw a more glorious life in front of me with the Salerno family.

It had an allure and mystique that pulled me away from any chance of ever having a legitimate life surrounded by regular people.

Over the following years, I came across more bullies as I climbed the Salerno family ladder.

Each time I faced one, I chose a more violent weapon than a simple pencil and my temper grew as well.

CARLO: In school, the bullies used to beat me up also. I was a small kid and not a good fighter. I learned how to deal with this by enlisting the largest bully to protect me and terrorize the other bullies.

I proposed an opportunity to him for us to make money together.

He agreed.

He stood behind me with a mean glare and his arms crossed as I pointed at him and warned another bully, "If you don't pay us $1 every day, then you will deal with him."

We convinced every bully to pay us every day. After school, we went to the racetrack and asked people to place bets for us.

This lasted for several months before my dad got a call from the school principal asking him to come by one afternoon and pick up his son.

The principal told my dad that his son was being expelled for extorting lunch money from the other students.

My father came to the school and yelled at me in front of the principal, "What are you thinking? Your behavior is terrible! How could you do this? You have embarrassed yourself and our family! What do you have to say for yourself?"

After I apologized, my dad gave the principal his sincerest apologies, and told him he would teach me a hard lesson.

Then, the principal agreed that I could return next year after I corrected my behavior.

When we reached my dad's car, he said, "If we hurry, we can catch the last two horse races at the racetrack!"

JOHNNY: Your dad was a character. I have a question for you.

What was it like to be homeless at your age?

CARLO: Even though I was homeless, I still hung out with my friends, but I felt too embarrassed to tell them I was homeless.

When they went home at night, I pretended to go home.

I had no one.

I learned to survive by going to grocery stores; stealing candy and bologna.

I went to a park nearby and ate them.

One day, the manager came from behind me and grabbed my arm, "Hey kid. I have been watching you for three weeks ripping my store off. You are in big trouble. Come with me."

We walked to his office at the front of the store. There you were sitting in the manager's office in the corner quietly counting money.

You looked up, and saw me sit down.

Then, you stood up, took the money with you, walked outside the office, and motioned for manager to join you.

The door closed behind both of you as you left the office.

Two minutes later, the manager came back into his office alone and brushed me off with, "Hey kid, take your stuff, and get out of here. Don't let me see you in here again. You got it?"

I never had the opportunity to thank you for that and many other things you did for me.

JOHNNY: No problem. Tell me what happened to your mother?

CARLO: Earlier this year, my mom started hanging out with a new boyfriend hooked on cocaine and heroin.

Soon enough, he hooked her on them as well.

The apartment where we lived went from being spotless, to being a real mess with dishes piling up, and nothing put away.

One evening, when they cuddled on the couch together, I stood in the hallway and overheard her boyfriend tell her, "We should get our own place, just you and me."

I couldn't hear how my mom responded.

I guess deep down I hoped she would yell at him and tell him to get lost, but I heard no such thing.

Afterwards, I stopped coming around my mom's place, and I moved in with my dad.

She overdosed a few months later.

JOHNNY: That's a shame. You have a new family now.

We'll take care of you.

Hey, whatever happened between your mom and dad to split them up?

CARLO: My earliest memories were happy. When I was five years old, my dad was a butcher, and my mom was a housewife.

My parents dressed me in the best clothes, and we went to church every Sunday. We enjoyed the zoo and carnivals as soon as they came to town. We were normal.

By the time I was nine years old, problems developed. My dad lost his job, and he joined a Brooklyn gang called the Eastside Boys.

JOHNNY: I heard of them. The gang is like a farm team for the mob. After a few years in the gang, we recruit the best guys.

CARLO: My mom didn't approve of dad's career change.

They began fighting all the time.

My mom would yell, "You are never home anymore! You hang out with those hoodlums! Is that your new goal in life? What kind of an example are you setting for our son!"

My dad would scream back, "I lost my job! You don't know anything! I need to make money! Besides, I don't need to threaten or hurt people, my reputation is enough!"

And then he would leave.

Before long, their fighting led to my dad moving out, and then my parents divorced.

I visited my dad on the weekends. On these visits, strange things would happen that I didn't understand.

He became hooked on drugs before my mom, but he managed it better.

I saw him strap a belt around his arm, and stick a needle in it. I thought he was taking medicine.

I didn't know it was heroin.

After taking it, he would disappear into his bedroom, and later he would wake up angry.

Then, he told me to get in the car so he could take me home.

On the drive, my dad stopped at a gas station and sternly told me, "Wait right here, don't say anything, and don't move."

I nodded my head and saw a quick glimpse of a gun stuffed in the back of his jeans.

I watched as my dad went inside the store, pulled out his .357 Magnum, and aimed it at the attendant behind the register.

The attendant nervously stuffed into a garbage bag all of the money in the cash register, cigarette cartons behind the counter, individual cigarette packs hanging above the register, and candy bars in front of the register.

Then, my dad quickly walked out, got into the car, and threw the bag in the back seat.

As he drove away, he reached into the bag for a stack of $20 bills and told me, "Give this to your mother."

JOHNNY: He gave you the money as a child support payment for your mom, correct?

CARLO: Yeah. Then, he reached into the bag again and gave me a handful of candy bars.

JOHNNY: Your dad was a bruiser and destined to be a very high ranking wiseguy, but his drug abuse became too much of a problem for him.

He became reckless with his robberies; brought too much heat from local cops, and the local wiseguys looked at him as a liability.

Things will work out better for you.

I guarantee it.

CARLO: Thanks, it already has. Despite my dad's problems, we still managed to have good times together like going to the horse races at the Aqueduct Track in Queens.

When we arrived at the track early, we went down to the horse stables and looked at the horses being walked around.

He asked me to identify little reasons why a horse had an edge on a given day by asking questions.

Did the horse and jockey look confident?

Did the horse appear healthy?

Did the horse prance when it walked?

Did it hold its head up high?

I would look at recent wins and losses of the jockeys and horses to identify any trends.

My dad asked me to pick the horses for each of the nine races that day.

After a while, I had an informed opinion on which horses and jockeys could beat the odds.

I told my dad, "This one is a winner. He had had a couple wins in the past three weeks; the odds don't take that into account. It's all in the race program."

The track drew over 20,000 people on big race days. People rushed from everywhere to place bets and find their seats before the first race started.

When we placed a bet, we felt excited, satisfied, thrilled and exhilarated. The immediate gratification from placing the bet was a rush. The more money we bet, the bigger the rush. If we won a bet, we felt another jolt of excitement.

At the end of the day, we took the train back home.

Most of the time, my dad would pass out in his seat right after we sat down.

This created an opportunity for me to stay on the train with him for a while and to marvel at the sites in Brooklyn, Harlem, Manhattan and Queens.

My eyes peered intently at the world outside, and I never tired of seeing everything.

A few times, we would stay on the train until close to midnight when my father woke up from being passed out asking, "Where are we?"

"Brooklyn, six more stops until our exit," I answered.

"What? How long have I been out of it?" My dad asked before he went back to sleep.

Around this time, I started skipping school to go to the track during the week. I liked placing bets, but I had no money, so I started coming up with hustles.

My idea for the first hustle came when I noticed people entered and left the races during the entire day.

After the first few races, some people lost their bets and stormed out of the racetrack mad.

As they exited the track, they threw their souvenir programs on the ground or in the garbage. The programs had statistics on the horse races for the day and cost $2.50 each.

I picked them up and sold them to people coming into the track at a discount for $1 each. When I did this, I made over a hundred dollars a day.

After a short time, one of the security guards grabbed me by the shoulders and told me to knock it off.

He asked me why I wasn't in school. I confided in him, "I'm hanging out here, how about you let me operate, and I give you 20%?"

He agreed and I kept the racetrack hustle going for a couple years.

The guard later told me he used the money I gave him to bet at the track.

He kept it a secret from his wife who controlled the money and didn't like him gambling.

JOHNNY: Interesting, kid.

Hey, we are in Queens. Take the exit at 103rd street coming up for my favorite bakery. Whenever I pass this bakery, I have to stop!

I buy every pie in the showcase next to the front register. I buy a pie for me and a pie for each boss to eat himself. The bosses love these pies. They all have diabetes.

Later, they go home and get sick. Their wives find out about the pies, and call my bar yelling, "Stop buying the pies! You're going to kill my husband!"

Whoever answers the phone at the bar answers, "Johnny keeps buying the pies! What do you want me to do?!"

Also, I buy the pepper and egg sandwiches and the tuna fish salad on fresh Italian bread. The bakery puts this Giardiniera sauce on the Italian bread that is so hot, it will make you sweat and laugh at the same time. It is to die for!

You're going to love this place, kid!

THE RIDE TO FLUKEY

Johnny sent me regularly to Schnaze's place to help him with different jobs. Schnaze entered the room talking in his crackly, gargled voice convoluted by 30 years of smoking weed and cigarettes.

To the untrained ear, Schnaze didn't sound like he spoke the English language. It sounded more like, "Rah, gargle, rah, oy, vey, gargle, cough, hack, gargle."

Schnaze, Lucky Charms and I left in his Bonneville driving from Clifton to Harlem. I was in the back seat as they conversed up front.

January 9, 2010

LUCKY: How was your holiday season?

SCHNAZE: I had a terrible holiday season, just terrible. A couple weeks before Christmas, I visited my dad at the nursing home.

When I walked in the front door, there was a horrible stench that made me fall to the ground.

My dad is only nice 10 days a year, and I'm never there for any of them.

When I saw him, he greeted me with, "The nurses cut my clothes off with a pair of scissors! The nurses have it in for me? I'm not safe here!"

I tried spending some time with him watching TV in his room.

He yelled at me during one of my favorite shows, "Why is it every time a crime show is on TV, your eyes light up? You were always into the monkey business! You believe it's not what you earn in pay per hour at a job; it's what you have the opportunity to steal! You're no good!"

My dad turned into a total whack job.

Unfortunately, his girlfriend, who is a nurse there, told me my dad was dying, and he needed to be moved to hospice care.

I pulled him out the following day.

On our drive to hospice, my dad yelled at me, "Did you rent this car?!"

"I own my car. Who rents a car that looks like mine with 250,000 miles?!" I told him.

I dropped him off at the hospice place. Three days later, he was dead.

I wrote a check to the funeral parlor.

It bounced.

They are suing me.

LUCKY: Sorry to hear about your dad.

SCHNAZE: It gets worse. I went through my dad's estate, and I found lots of bills from a rip-off repairman that one of my sisters paid for my dad while he was in the nursing home.

One of the bills charged my dad $4,000 to replace a dining room ceiling fan.

I went to the dining room to see this fan. I thought this must be one hell of a fan!

The fan looked like it came from someone's garbage pile with two of the four fan blades broken off and dust all over it.

The repairman was a fake and a phony!

As I look back and reflect on my Dad's final years, it was all downhill for him after he shacked up with the hillbilly old lady, who is the mother of Giovanni's mother.

He tried to look good for her by getting a gut reduction and liposuction, despite the fact that he was 74 years old.

He had no business having the surgery in the first place!

After the surgery, the doctor prescribed him oxycodone for his recovery and he was hooked.

His health deteriorated from the drug abuse!

The more I dug, the more I found this hillbilly melted my dad down for most of his entire life savings.

I discovered a stack of bills for her that my dad paid which included her new boobs, her new teeth, her liposuction, her diamond jewelry, her designer clothes, and her numerous vacations to Poland.

I felt sick when I was done going through everything.

The rip-off repairman took the rest of the money leftover!

LUCKY: How about Christmas? Did you have a good Christmas?

SCHNAZE: Christmas was terrible.

My two sisters, their boyfriends, and my sisters' kids came over Christmas evening.

My sisters smelled like insect repellant with their cheap perfume and hairspray.

Every year, never fail, they expect me to pay for all the Christmas food, buy Christmas presents for their lousy, spoiled kids, buy presents for whomever their boyfriend is for that year, and they always leave my house a complete mess.

I'm getting fed up with it!

My one sister is fortunate to be alive. She is a bank teller in Jersey City. The week before Christmas a customer came into her bank. He whispered to her what she thought was, "Where's my wallet?"

But what he really said was, "Where's the vault?"

He had a gun in his pocket pointed at her that she didn't see.

Oblivious to the bank robber's intentions, she looked at him like he was an imbecile and ordered him to sit down in the waiting area on a couch in the middle of the bank.

She looked into answering his question with the other bank employees and busily asked each employee behind the counter, "Have you seen that man's wallet?"

The bank robber fidgeted and looked agitated.

She couldn't figure out why, so she told him sternly, "Look, Mister, I'm trying to help you. You could show a little appreciation."

He muttered under his breath, "Bitch."

He flashed his gun at her, and she realized his true intentions. Now it was her turn to fidget, but then he left.

My other sister is no better.

She's the dingbat who took a fireman to her high school senior prom.

She was 18. He was 28.

He looked like he was 45, had a beard, chain-smoked, and drank too much.

There are old pictures before the prom of my dad and him at the kitchen table smoking and drinking.

The prom picture showed this creep hanging his arm over my sister's shoulder with his hand cupping her breast.

Years later, I asked my mom, "How could you let such an older guy date your daughter?"

My mom responded she was proud her daughter dated a fireman, and that my dad was much older than the fireman when he took her to her prom years ago.

God rest her soul.

Later, on Christmas evening, I went outside for a smoke with my sister.

I found out the boyfriend she brought with her this year had five grown children from previous marriages, and all five were on her cell phone family plan along with him.

I told her, "He's taking advantage of you."

She said, "He helps me around the house with repairs. Also, he did a lot of work on dad's house before he died."

I went ballistic and fumed, "Are you telling me your boyfriend is the rip-off repairman?"

The smoke break was over.

I found her boyfriend inside, asked him to step outside where I confronted him.

We were fighting and rolling around in the snow.

One of my sister's kids looked out the window at us and yelled to the other six kids in the house, "Hey, Uncle Schnaze is making snow angels with Mom's boyfriend!"

The kids ran outside making snow angels near us. What a sight it must have been.

LUCKY: Your family's holiday together sounded like a traveling Italian-gypsy circus.

SCHNAZE: Fuck you. Anyways, I never had the opportunity to ask my sister if she knew about or took part in her boyfriend's scam.

If she did, I would be furious!

LUCKY: You wouldn't believe what Johnny did to me as a prank on New Year's Eve.

I was passed out upstairs. He sneaked in my garage at 3am, and he started eight brand new Honda snow blowers that I had boosted from the local home improvement store.

Then, he opened the door inside my garage connected to the inside of my house, and the snow blowers blew smoke and carbon monoxide everywhere.

My whole place smelled like a gas refinery. I could have died.

Next, I was awakened by a loud boom in my front yard that shook the house.

It felt like a seismic earthquake and sounded like an electrical transfer station exploded.

To wake me up, Johnny put a stick, yes, an entire stick of dynamite, in my mailbox at the end of my driveway.

My neighbor across the street said the flash from the blast lit her bedroom and made her think lightning had struck my house.

She just had newborn twins whom she was rocking to sleep.

Both of her newborns wailed from the scary, loud noise.

SCHNAZE: Eventually, I want to take some time and enjoy life. Find a woman I can eventually settle down with. You know what I mean?

LUCKY: No, I don't. There are two things I've never seen: a UFO and a bitch I need.

SCHNAZE: That's cold my brother. You have real feelings that are deeper than that. I know you do.

LUCKY: I've never met a woman where I said, "I know I'm not the first man you ever kissed, but I want to be the last." I want to feel that way. I just haven't.

SCHNAZE: You've been hurt too many times.

LUCKY: Maybe you're right. As you know, I've tried dating women, but I tend to attract bullies in a relationship.

SCHNAZE: The bully loves her punching bag. Hang in there. Speaking of women, how is your new girlfriend?

LUCKY: She is globe-style round, long hair, tits, and cutoff biker vest like a man would wear, concrete expert, master Bobcat operator and knows how to repair small engines.

Her ex-boyfriend is the head of the Camden, NJ chapter of the Outlaws Biker Gang.

She could help us on our construction jobs.

You want to hear a joke?

A guy goes to his doctor complaining he has an orange dick.

The doctor does a bunch of tests and tells the guy everything appears to be normal.

Then, the doctor says to the guy, "Do you mind if I ask you what you do in your leisure time?"

This may help me diagnose the source of your problem.

The guy says he watches porno all day and eats Cheetos.

SCHNAZE: Funny. Hey, we just passed 125th street where the bus station is located and hookers with bullet-hole scars solicit on the corner.

We're getting close to the heroin drop. We have a little time.

LUCKY: I'll tell you about a guy I know who just bought property in Albania.

SCHNAZE: Isn't it corrupt out there?

LUCKY: What's wrong with that? Nowhere in the world is more corrupt than the United States.

At least in Albania you can afford to buy your way out of any problems.

The cops ride on donkeys, and you can purchase a woman for a bushel of oranges.

When I retire, I want to live in Atlantic City.

I have a friend who has a job as a host at one of the big casinos.

He brings VIP guests to the hotel and plans their weekends for them.

The host puts together a package like free rooms, free flights, free limos, free dinners, free shows, free nightclubs, etc.

The host is paid by earning 20% of the VIP guest losses. The more his guests lose, the more he earns!

The casinos have no problem giving 20% of a gambler's losses to a host because they keep the other 80%.

On top of that, the casinos give a free room in the hotel for their hosts to live.

Can you imagine?

Based on how much a VIP guest loses, the casinos assign a rating to the guest that they share with each other.

A host from any of the hotels can look up anybody.

SCHNAZE: Ask your friend if he can look us up, we must have the highest VIP rating.

LUCKY: We don't stay at the big hotels so we are not in their databases.

I figure if I can get hired by a casino and invite my contacts, most of them are high rollers like us, and are out for long weekend vacations. I could live like a king on 20% of their losses.

SCHNAZE: You could live like a king on my losses alone.

LUCKY: Ok, we're here. I'll park at the end of the alley and leave the car running.

Kid, you move up front to the driver's seat and watch us.

Long story short, the drug dealer from Chicago named Flukey might want us dead.

We supply his guys with a lot of heroin that we buy from the Salerno's.

Recently, Flukey's guys have been getting robbed on their drives to Chicago.

Flukey could be blaming us, but we had nothing to do with those robberies.

I wish we never got into drug dealing.

With drugs, we meet too many rough and violent characters that get all coked up and can't control themselves.

They pull out their guns and go crazy, nuts.

They don't think straight.

The dealers' minds are mush from the drugs.

End of conversation dated January 9, 2010

This was my first drug deal. I was anxious, but I didn't show it. Schnaze and Lucky Charms left the car, met their contacts in the alley, and exchanged brown paper bags. A car emerged from the opposite end of the alley, sped toward them, and stopped. Two men got out, flashed badges, drew their guns, and screamed, "DEA! Everyone put your hands in the air and get down on the ground now!"

Everyone went down on the ground.

One cop yelled, "Where is the paper? Straight up, we don't play games! Time for a donation or we kill you! We don't give a fuck! We rob drug dealers as a community service!"

This was when I thought, "Damn, these mother fuckers may not be the police, now what?"

The fake cops grabbed the heroin and the money.

Flukey's guys started shooting.

The fake cops fired back.

Schnaze and Lucky ran down the alley toward our car.

As they ran, Schnaze held up his pants that kept falling down, and Lucky kept one hand on his toupee so it wouldn't blow off.

Both Schnaze and Lucky had flesh wounds on their backs.

I took them to the hospital where they recovered.

Rumor was the two fake cops were the ones who robbed Flukey's recent drug shipments.

Flukey ordered the two fake cops dead, but not before Flukey ended up dead as well.

The Feds broke up the Salerno family heroin business by sending the top guys who ran it to jail for 50 years.

Schnaze and Lucky weren't charged on the case.

THE ART EXPERT

When I was young, I thought Thomas Flanagan was one of the most magnetic personalities I ever met. He had a different background from other guys I knew who patronized Johnny's bar. He journeyed extensively throughout the world, and he told the most unique stories that took me places where I had never been.

As he would talk for hours at a time, my eyes widened with wonder and my mouth hung agape. A portion of our first conversation together is highlighted below:

January 18, 2010

CARLO: Where did you grow up?

FLANAGAN: I grew up in the old section of Greenwich, CT. Both my mother and father's families are in the art business. My mother's family is from England, the Billingsleys.

They own art auction houses throughout Europe in Paris, Berlin, Rome, London, and New York City. My father's family owns the Flanagan art auction houses of the east and west coasts.

I was lucky and fortunate to be born into such a wealthy and connected family.

Kids from my neighborhood where I grew up didn't have normal names. We have two middle names. One middle name is to highlight which dead president, dead banker or other famous person from which we are descended.

My full name is Thomas Adam Billingsley Flanagan. Billingsley is obviously after my mother's side of the family. My first wife was named Michele Ann Roosevelt Smith.

She was related to former President Franklin Delano Roosevelt. Up and down the east coast, people have these long names to distinguish themselves from everybody else.

My eighteen cousins and I are all part of a trust from our Grandfather Billingsley. I took over investments made by the trust several years ago and doubled the annual payments to $500,000 for each recipient.

Do you think I get even a "thank You" from any of my cousins? No, but they sure enjoy the larger checks!

When I was growing up, it wasn't uncommon for Andy Warhol to have dinner at our house or the Shah of Iran to drop by when he was in town.

My parents sold Andy Warhol's paintings at their auctions, and the Shah bought a lot of art from my parents.

Imelda Marcos was a client.

My parents knew everybody who was anybody back then, and I met them all through my parents. I had the best jobs as a young guy due to my connections.

The most fun I ever had as a young guy was when I owned a Manhattan club during the 1990s. It was where movie stars and rock stars went to party in New York City. I danced with

Claudia Schiffer, hung out with Kurt Cobain, partied with Arnold Schwarzenhegger, and tried to hit on Cindy Crawford. I found them to be normal people like you and I.

CARLO: Wow. What is it like to be in the art business?

FLANAGAN: Here's the thing. I'm a dealmaker. I put together art deals. A few years ago, Mexican drug dealers showed up at my auction house with bags of money over their shoulder asking for $6 million in art.

Even drug dealers know art is a great investment if you can stay with it for the long term. I was more than happy to help them out.

I'll tell you a little about how my auction business works.

In a good economy, I may offer 80 pieces at an auction, and most will sell. I make money on both sides of the sale, 10% from the buyer, and 10% from the seller.

On a $1 million piece of art that sells at my auction, I make $200,000.

In a good economy, the majority of my clients are the latest millionaires from Manhattan or Silicon Valley.

I call them the newly rich. They always want a painting by a famous artist like Picasso. You may remember in the news a few years back a Picasso sold for a record $26 million.

When my clients heard about the Picasso, they called me. They wanted the bragging rights to boast to their friends, "I own a Picasso!"

What they didn't know, realized or cared to research was not all Picassos are priced the same, and some are worth a lot more than others.

At the time, I had a less popular Picasso offered at my auction for $1 million and my newly rich clients thought it was a deal. A few of them bid the price up to the point where the winner acquired it for $2 million.

Eighteen months later, a recession hit the economy.

The newly rich of the good economy became the newly poor. They were never prepared for a slump because they never experienced one, and they overextended themselves.

The same guy who bought the Picasso for $2 million visited me with his face twisted in agony.

He told me his businesses were in trouble, and his expenses were out of control.

He confessed he didn't need his penthouse in New York, his beachfront house in Florida, his multiple boats and his numerous exotic cars.

Quite frankly, nobody does.

He admitted with a look of dread, "I need to sell my Picasso; I'll take whatever I can get for it."

This was music to my ears, but I kept it real and stated the truth, "Right now isn't a good time to sell. If you can wait 12 months, you will do better. Today, everybody is selling, and very few people are buying. Paintings will only trade for below wholesale.

I have 200 paintings like yours offered at my next auction, and, regrettably, most won't sell.

At best, I can only get $300,000 for your Picasso. I'm sorry."

For a moment, he gawked and convulsed, then understanding crossed his face as his head dropped, "Please sell it now."

I sympathized with him. Over my career, I have observed this scenario play out hundreds of times with other people.

Like I told him I would, I peddled his Picasso for $300,000. I may be immoral, but this is why I love the art business.

For his one painting, I made money on both sales of the same art piece. I made $200,000 off the original sale price of $1 million, and $60,000 off the $300,000 selling price, for a total of $260,000, not bad for one painting!

The key lesson here is when the economy goes up and down, I make most of my money from the newly rich and their foolishness.

People who have always had money can afford to buy art regardless of where the economy stands.

I call these people old money. They are smarter with how they spend their money, and that is why they always have it.

Do you know what I enjoy the most about my business? It is when economies collapse, like The Soviet Union did many years ago. Everything, and I mean everything, was for sale at big discounts.

I flew my private jet and a briefcase full of cash.

My rules were: I come, I pay, and I leave with the goods, very simple.

The first guy I met in Moscow was an Admiral from the Soviet Union's Navy who tried to sell me one of the battleships from his fleet.

A real battleship is the size of five football fields!

It was the most ridiculous thing I had the opportunity to buy in my career.

It probably cost billions to build, but he only wanted $4 million for it!

CARLO: A real battleship for $4 million?

FLANAGAN: Yeah, he insisted on giving me a tour of the ship. He would have had me there all day if I didn't cut the tour short.

I didn't have time to waste and buying a battleship wasn't practical.

He looked at me confused.

I asked the Admiral a bunch of rhetorical questions, "What would make you think I am in the market for a battleship? What can I do with one?"

He swallowed hard and gave me a blank gaze.

Let's say I bought it. What would happen when I cruise it across the Atlantic Ocean? What if I bumped into a U.S. Coast Guard or U.S. Navy warship on the way or outside New York City?

If they didn't fire and sink me first before I had a chance to explain myself, what would you recommend I say?

I can imagine a U.S. Navy person giving me a sidelong curious look, and asking me where I got this ship?

What should I say?

I can't tell him, "My friend, a Soviet Admiral, sold it to me."

I can't give him a bill of sale or a legal title like I could if I bought a car.

The $4 million I would pay the Admiral doesn't go to the Soviet government, the money goes in the Admiral's pockets!

Another problem is how would I dock and register a battleship as a boat in the U.S.?

I did him a favor and made some calls to see if I could pull together a deal to help him out.

The only option I discovered for him was to set sail for Finland or Sweden where I could connect him with someone who could sell the ship for scrap metal.

He could make a $20 million profit!

Another one of my rules is if something mechanical is for sale over there, it usually doesn't work.

No matter what promises they make.

In China, it's a little different story.

When I try to buy something there, it will probably work, but it is never what they say it is.

I never buy anything from China unless I am standing on the factory floor while they manufacture the product.

I need to see it or no deal.

CARLO: If you didn't buy the battleship, what did you buy while you were in the Soviet Union?

FLANAGAN: After meeting with the Admiral, I had a separate meeting with two young KGB officials, Alexei Dobrinov and Vasili Zhukov.

They grew up in East Berlin because their parents worked for the Soviet Union government.

Their life and their home was in East Berlin.

They felt stranded and abandoned by the USSR right before and after the collapse. They did what they could to survive the tumultuous time by offering me the opportunity of a lifetime to buy paintings from legendary artists such as Picasso, Edgar Degas, Henri Matisse, Paul Gauguin, Rembrandt, and Vincent Van Gogh.

They met me in Leningrad, which is now called St Petersburg.

They had special access to an art and culture museum called the Hermitage.

The Hermitage is one of the largest and oldest museums in the world and has been open to the public since 1852. It has the largest collection of paintings in the world. There are over three million items at the museum, and most of the items are kept not on public display, but stored in the basement.

Dobrinov and Zhukov were nervous about doing the deal, and they took big risks in meeting with me.

When I arrived, Dobrinov skittishly told me, "Mr. Flanagan, our employees here at the Hermitage have not been paid in three months. There is little confidence in our government. Many are predicting a collapse."

They escorted me hastily down to the museum basement which had thousands of boxed art pieces with an inch of dust on them from decades of storage.

The pieces were stacked against the walls fifteen deep.

I tried to put them at ease by trying to make conversation, "Where did all of these pieces come from?"

Dobrinov informed me, "Much of the stored art you see is from the last war, World War Two, confiscated from the Nazis as war reparations for their crimes against our Mother Russia. Other pieces are from the collection of the last Tsar of Russia, Tsar Nicholas, who was over thrown as part of the people's revolution of 1917 that was the birth of communism and helped end World War I."

I asked him what was for sale, and he responded it was all negotiable.

I thought, "What a score!"

Then, Dobrinov's partner, Zhukov, jumped in tightening his jaw with a hesitant scowl, "There are government spies and informants everywhere here in Leningrad. We have maybe one hour before we can expect the police to arrive and inquire as to why you are here. We have a boat waiting at the loading dock that can carry at least 50 pieces. Please select what you want. The boat will take you to your airfield three miles away with safe transport to Finland. We have other people that want to speak with you about your next trip."

They both loaded the art on a speedboat, and I gave them $2 million in cash.

They joined me for the short journey to a port near the airfield where my jet awaited.

Zhukov clutched my hand reverently and his forehead beaded with sweat as he said, "You have helped many families here make it through the upcoming winter."

I asked them what they planned to do with their portion of the money.

Dobrinov revealed his plans to immigrate to New York City, and I offered my help with his transition. He accepted, and he recently moved to Brooklyn as a business owner.

I found Zhukov to be much more interesting with his plans. As he described them, it was not the words he chose to use, but the passion and energy in which he spoke them that intrigued me.

Before we left the dock on a boat with the paintings, I had a conversation with him.

Zhukov started off with a history lesson. He declared, "In order for us to look forward, please allow me to take a look back, to the time of the ancient Romans, when they ruled most of Europe. The Roman leaders built the most advanced, cultured society. It was centuries ahead of anyone else in the world. The Romans had teachers, doctors, craftsman, artists, actors, theologists, philosophers, and politicians. Their buildings were magnificent, sophisticated, ornate, and made of stone with running water brought in by massive aqueducts.

The rest of the world lived in mud huts, crouched around fires in their bare feet, and had no culture or civilized existence. They were the most backward, barbarian heathens you can imagine, and that's an understatement!

The point I am trying to make is the Romans should have done the rest of the world a favor and conquered the rest of humanity in order to civilize it. In fact, it was their duty and responsibility. However, this could not be achieved. The Romans lacked the technology to travel across the globe. They did not know how to build boats that could carry their armies to the furthest destinations necessary, and to create vehicles on land for the same purposes.

My movement will travel unimpeded in the coming years throughout the digital world. I will lead and develop a movement that will be based on technology. Due to our superior technology, and without anyone knowing it, my movement will clandestinely conquer every government, large and small. I will someday sit humbly before you and everyone else in the world as the sole leader for all humanity."

I asked him, "How is your movement better than what exists today?"

He explained, "I am not alone in feeling contempt for all persons and events who have enabled the shabby current world order of things. You can see it everywhere. Power is held by the corrupt, privileged few who subjugate, for their own benefit, the masses of humanity. There are too many wars, too much petty bickering, false rhetoric, lies, fraudulent schemes, divisiveness, debts that are impossible to repay, and bloated governments. Humanity faces inevitable annihilation on a number of fronts. Whether it be from the endless pollution that will eventually destroy the planet, to inadequate, poor economies that offer no good jobs or prospects for a better life. It is all destined to implode!

Most people today accept this current order of things. I reject it!

I must stop and hold accountable the swine who created this mess and show them no mercy!

Nonetheless, I am not naïve enough to assume there will not be a fight. There will be those who seek to stall or disrupt my movement. Victory without loss of blood is impossible. We will be prepared and ready.

Many would say my movement is doomed, or that my movement's objective to rule the world is too bold. I will not accept such talk!

We must win our war to liberate humanity!"

I had a strange captivation in hearing this. I craved to hear more, "How will you do this?"

He illuminated further, "First, we will seize control of the economies and infrastructure of the largest countries grinding them to a halt. I am talking about all of their banking, power grids, satellites, weapon systems, and other infrastructures. I will develop the technology to accomplish this.

Then, with minimal effort, we will liberate the exploited third world countries from their painful existence. We will redistribute wealth on a global scale. The third world will welcome our efforts with enthusiasm and glee.

Lastly, from the worldwide chaos, we will emerge as the only legitimate option for government and guarantors of safety and security for everyone.

My plans will progress faster than I expect.

In the coming decades, new events will unfold to activate what I just described.

As I look to the future, my plans extend long after my death. I will find young leaders, who can carry out my plans long after I am gone to continue to control the world's power from those who seek to misuse it.

Do you support my movement and stand with me, or will you stand with the swine who are firmly against me?"

I shook myself out of a gaze.

Did he want me to answer him? I never met anyone who could speak like this.

I didn't have the opportunity to give him my thoughts.

Within moments after we left the dock, there was a hail of machine gun bullets firing at us from a police boat behind us. My head jerked backwards from Dobrinov opening the engine to full redline as he weaved the boat in the water to avoid the gunfire and evade capture.

Zhukov's face grimaced with fury as he fired back with his own machine gun.

I'm thinking, "I didn't sign up for this!"

I hid behind a tarp and peered out. The firefight continued.

The police boat gained on us.

Seconds later, there was a massive explosion.

The police boat took a direct hit and sunk. I watched the burning fire in the distance against the early evening setting sun blazing down on the water.

After that episode, the Soviet Union indicted me in absentia as an enemy of the state, and then the country collapsed.

I was never able to return and buy more art!

The women in the Soviet Union are something else.

A friend of mine went over there a couple years ago and lucked out meeting a gorgeous woman.

I have to tell you, my friend is ugly, and he couldn't get a date with an American girl to save his life.

She was a heart surgeon who spoke English. He married her.

She moved to be with him here in New York, and she made more than him as a doctor!

He told me she wakes him up every morning with a blowjob.

What a perfect wife, I thought. My next wife will be Russian.

American wives don't do that because they are too entitled and spoiled.

CARLO: Aren't you being a little too hard on American women?

FLANAGAN: Not really. Do you know when I asked my second ex-wife what she would do if I had a stroke or was mentally disabled; she said she would find a home for me.

I questioned her, "Really? A home? What about caring for me or nursing me back to health?"

She had the same approach with me as with her own mother who she was arranging to dump in a nursing home.

I offered, "Why don't we have your mother move in with us? We have 13,000 square feet in our townhouse. We could give your mother her own floor. We wouldn't even notice her."

My ex-wife said her mother would be too much of a burden. Can you believe it?

That is the problem with American women!

They are too pampered.

My ex-wife has a career if you can call it one. She started out as a TV broadcaster in Atlanta and was recruited to work for a station here in New York. She does the weekend evening news.

Our townhouse was in a magnificent four story pre-war building right on Fifth Avenue and faced Central Park. I used to take our dog for a walk from 65th to 71st street three times a day.

My ex-wife would never take the dog for a walk!

Even though we are divorced, we still get along. Of course, I gave her the townhouse in the divorce settlement.

I bought a townhouse down the street from her. I still see her when I take the dog for a walk sometimes.

CARLO: Understood. You said you buy precious metals, where do you buy those?

FLANAGAN: I buy them primarily on the west coast of Africa where the leaders of local tribes broker the deals.

These are smaller deals, but there are always risks.

I never bring more than $250,000 in cash with me because the customs office or the local police will get word of the cash I am carrying and try to rob me at some point during the trip.

Also, I buy precious stones. Here's a story.

Through a friend I knew in Australia, I heard about $3 million worth of red rubies available to purchase for only $500,000 in cash from a senior Cambodian government official.

Cambodia is still a third world country with lots of unrest and instability. Being a part of the government there can be a risky endeavor with plenty of assassinations.

They take steps to protect themselves. I had been going there for years.

My Australian friend spoke Cambodian and flew with me on my jet.

When we landed, a military truck escorted us down several winding roads for a couple hours until we reached a large white mansion on a plantation in the middle of a rain forest.

CARLO: Government jobs must pay well there.

FLANAGAN: Here's the thing with government leaders in third world countries. The more they can steal, the more they make. Mr. Tranh asked us to keep our meeting secret and discreet, which is code for, "I'm selling you stuff I stole."

When I met with him and reviewed the rubies, I realized I could only sell them for about $1.8 million. I thanked him for the opportunity to review the fine stones, but I awkwardly declined buying them for $500,000 and attempted to renegotiate our deal.

Mr. Tranh crossed his arms, leaned forward and was adamant on the $500,000 amount. He proposed he could acquire more rubies in a couple months to make up the difference, and he asked if this was agreeable to me.

I pointed out, "Mr. Tranh, I am in the transaction business, not the credit business. Our deal is cash for stones. I can also do cash for raw materials, like precious metals, gold or silver. "

His eyes lit up as he asked, "How about we make up the difference with heroin? It is 100% pure. You consider this a raw material, correct?"

I bolstered myself and gave him a heartfelt stare, "Mr. Tranh, I primarily deal in art, and I do these types of deals on the side. I am not a drug dealer, nor am I a drug distributor or trafficker. I would be interested if you have any other raw materials available?"

He shrugged and said, "I have sugar, mountains of it, but Americans love our heroin."

I was getting concerned when I asked him, "Mr. Tranh, I have no doubt that your heroin is of the utmost quality, but I politely decline. Do you have anything else besides sugar or heroin?"

That is when Mr. Tranh gave me a response that knocked me off my feet, "I have people, lots of people, $5,000 a head. You supply the boat. 200 people a load. $1 million cash per load."

I explained, "Mr. Tranh, I am a legitimate business man. I am not a human trafficker.

What you propose is a serious crime in my country."

He said with a scowl, "Mr. Flanagan, to get to places you have never been sometimes requires for you to do things you have never done."

I could sense the deal was going to a bad place. In these situations, I can't apply pressure and bring him to heal because I am in his country as a visitor.

I tried to save the deal by telling him, "I do not mean to offend you, but, no thank you. Back to our original deal, I can adjust my price for the rubies to $300,000 in cash today. Do you agree?"

Tranh took an angry posture and muttered, "You Americans are always trying to renegotiate an agreement to your advantage. You probably view me as a banana republic mental midget.

How do I know that my rubies are not worth $3 million? By taking your word for it? I tried being open and flexible with you, no more; it is time for me to go. Have a nice day!"

Tranh briskly left the room. My partner and I looked at each other clueless. The rubies remained on the table. I reached for my briefcase full of the cash and sauntered toward the room exit. The butler escorted us to the car.

Then, rifle rounds landed inches from our feet fired by two guards standing at front door of the house. Between the guards, Tranh appeared with a snide look and threw the bag of rubies at me, "Gentlemen, please leave your money, here are your jewels."

A guard ran up, grabbed my briefcase, and exchanged it for the jewels.

As we boarded my jet, I told my friend to take a look at the view, because this would be our last trip to Cambodia. Not all of the deals I put together work out perfectly as I would like.

Although, in this case, when I sold the rubies here in the States, I did make over $1.3 million in profit that I split with my partner!"

MASTER OF THE FLY DUMP

I knocked on the door and walked into Schnaze's house. In the living room, there was a white towel laid on a dirty couch with a cute lady dressed in a negligée on it. In Schnaze's house, laying a clean white towel on the furniture meant creating a protective layer between you and the filth.

Schnaze and Lucky Charms were in the backyard. I found them and we climbed inside one of the trucks to head to a job.

May 21, 2010

> SCHNAZE: I think we should buy a strip club.
>
> LUCKY: Are you out of your mind? Owning a strip club is awful with nothing but problems. I hear every day the cops demand bribe payments, and expect free lap dances and blowjobs in a private room.
>
> If you don't pay them, the cops bust you for prostitution.
>
> On top of that, among the customers, there are fights every night over the women who smash beer glasses and break furniture.
>
> Did you know it takes the average stripper 90 to 120 days before they get strung out on methamphetamines and their teeth turn brown and black and start to fallout?
>
> The strippers transform into the foulest and most nauseating of women. They didn't start out that way though.

SCHNAZE: When did you become such an authority on strip clubs?

LUCKY: I'm not. Flanagan introduced me to a Russian guy named Alexei Dobrinov. He lives in Brooklyn, the Brighton Beach neighborhood. He bought almost all the strip clubs last month.

Dobrinov is now connected to Johnny to keep the local cops off his back.

I supply Dobrinov's clubs with meth, cocaine, weed, and other stuff.

SCHNAZE: Take me with you next time you make a delivery, I want to meet this guy and his ladies.

Last week, Johnny chastised me for being broke again. He asked me why I don't buy a new car with the money he gives me. I told him I like my car. The motor is good.

Enough talking, we have to get going to the fly dump I planned. Let's all jump in my truck.

Hey kid, today I need you to help me with a problem I have. Last week, I moved 20 truckloads of garbage from a construction site for a builder of mansions in Upper Saddle River, New Jersey.

He told me he couldn't afford to pay me until after the mansions were built, which meant I needed to wait three months.

He frustrated me. Did the builder forget if I didn't clear the garbage out, he wouldn't have been able to build the houses? This isn't gambling where I can afford to provide people credit because I have no hard costs.

Then, I hear the concrete guys who poured the foundations received a certified check that day. In addition, I find out the gravel guys who do work before the concrete guys were paid with a certified check as well. This annoyed me.

Does the builder think I'm some kind of jerkoff? Why can't I be paid like the others? It's unfair. I have real costs that I already paid like paying the garbage dump to take the builder's trash. Also, I paid my drivers to load their trucks and dump the garbage.

And the builder lies to me and says he can't afford to pay me? My invoice for the job to him was fifteen thousand dollars.

I gave him a bargain in the first place and I charged him a fraction of what the concrete and gravel guys charged. You see what I'm saying?

Today, I'm going to send the builder a message.

You're going to help me with it.

We're going to visit the builder's job site.

It's Saturday morning and no one will be there.

Here's the plan. Take this cell phone. I'll drop you off at the end of the street to stand guard. You're going to watch for any cars while I call some of my friends who have trucks like me.

We're going to dump 100 truckloads of garbage and some salvage yard junk cars inside the freshly poured foundations of the builder's houses. We're hitting the builder with what I call a "fly dump."

Hey kid, did you like the McCluck I had over at my house?

CARLO: McCluck?

SCHNAZE: Yes, the McCluck. I'll explain. A lot of young gals are what I call weed-heads. I don't understand why they allow themselves to get so dependent on weed.

They let their entire life revolve around an ounce of weed a week, which makes about 30 joints.

It's a $500-$750 a week habit.

They'll do anything to support their habit, and I mean anything.

They're whores.

I have a fleet of them, just like my trucks. When you get older, I'll introduce you to some of them.

LUCKY: Why don't you tell us about the last McCluck you chose to be your bride?

SCHNAZE: Fuck off.

LUCKY: Schnaze's wedding was at a run-down little chapel near the main strip in Las Vegas.

It seemed like he invited every mosquito and fly in the city.

At the ceremony, there was a foot pump organ that played what sounded like horror movie music as a limousine with no muffler pulled up in front of the chapel to drop off Schnaze and his McCluck bride to be married by an Elvis impersonator.

SCHNAZE: After the wedding, we honeymooned at a secluded Caribbean island hotel.

I complained about the nude beach jammed full of overweight Europeans outside our ground floor room window and patio area.

For our first breakfast buffet together, we went to the hotel restaurant.

There were no other restaurants nearby except the one in the hotel.

The restaurant had two dining areas separated by a wall of glass: one dining area outside for nude beach customers, and the other dining area inside the hotel for clothed customers.

The hostess seated us inside at a table in a corner with a direct view of an old man outside with everything on display.

I told the hostess this was our honeymoon, and

I requested to be moved to one of the open tables away from the view of the nude beach.

The hostess copped an attitude and snapped at me, "Those tables are reserved. I'm sorry, but you'll have to stay where you are."

After the honeymoon, I called my credit card company shouting that I wanted a full refund of all charges by the hotel.

After six months of numerous phone calls and letters, my card company reversed the charges.

LUCKY: It wasn't long after the honeymoon that Schnaze caught his McCluck soliciting herself to his friends to support her new crack habit.

I wasn't one of her customers.

They rode her in abandoned cars and alleyways.

When Schnaze found out and confronted her about it, he was furious.

When she expanded her customer base to strangers, she was arrested and sent to jail for three years.

SCHNAZE: Why couldn't she stop smoking crack? For me, it was harder to stop smoking cigarettes than to stop smoking crack.

Giovanni was just getting attached to her as his new stepmom.

Enough about my problems, I am going to signal on my CB radio to all the truckers I know that a free garbage dropoff point for a limited time is available at the builder's site.

You mark my words; there will 100 trucks here in one hour.

CARLO: Where does all the garbage come from?

SCHNAZE: Are you kidding me? You wouldn't believe how much garbage is being hauled around at any time in this city.

Let me tell you something. For a $15,000 unpaid bill, the builder will now have $75,000 worth of garbage and salvage yard cars sitting inside the new foundations of his 15 houses.

The builder can't move forward until he gets all the garbage hauled away.

Guess who will receive the call from the builder on Monday to move all the garbage?

Who else? Me.

I'll require payment of the old $15,000 bill and pre-payment of the $75,000 bill for the cleanup. The builder has no choice but to pay.

I earned my nickname, "The Master of the Fly Dump."

Hey kid, what kinds of crimes do you do when you are not with us or Johnny?

CARLO: Stealing Cadillacs is my favorite way to make easy money. I sell the bumpers to an auto body shop for $100 each and they give me $85 for the radio.

All I need is a large Philips screwdriver and an open end socket wrench. I take a rock, break the driver's side window, crawl inside through the window, pry open the bottom portion of the steering column with a screwdriver, pulled the ignition cord in the column, and the car starts.

The steering wheel is in the locked position because no key has been inserted. I brake the steering wheel column lock with a couple of hard tugs.

Next, I drive the Cadillac to a parking where I began removing the four bolts on the bumper and a couple screws for the radio. I can remove a radio in under a minute.

I leave the car in the lot when I am done.

Last month, I heard a crew from outside of our neighborhood moved in and stole cars at an alarming rate.

A lot of the kids who do the car stealing in our neighborhood are from the Salerno family. We all feel that if anyone is going to steal from our neighborhood, it has to be us, not an outsider.

Therefore, eight of us quietly patrolled the streets at night looking for the car thieves. A few nights later, we found them, gave them a good beating, and chased them off.

SCHNAZE: Good job kid, way to protect your neighborhood!

CARLO: Another thing I do for side money is take the bus to Manhattan to buy wholesale perfume from Delancey Street.

Most of the shops there sell hot merchandise at super discount prices. People drive from all over the tri-state area to buy stuff there.

I buy bottles of Polo or Drakkar Cologne for $15 and take them back to the Queens and sell them to small shop owners for $30, who would sell it to their customers for $40, which is $10 under what the department stores sell it for.

MULE ESCAPADES

When I entered the drug game in 2010, the drugs were dropped off in Florida where they would be picked up and distributed all over the country. Schnaze and Lucky Charms outgrew their local New York contacts and developed a direct contact with a Cartel guy in Florida early that year.

In the beginning, they were the ones driving down to Florida to do the drug pickups and driving back to New York to sell it. I came with them on a few trips. For the drive, they used cars with big trunks like Cadillacs and Lincolns. After they sold a trunk load in New York, they flew down to Florida to pay their Colombian contact the cost for the drugs.

Often, they stayed in Florida a few extra days and enjoyed the beach before flying back to New York. For a while, this setup worked with no problems.

Yet after taking these trips, they were gone from New York a lot.

This resulted in Johnny asking questions about where they were, and they had to figure out something that could work better for the long term.

They needed someone to do these trips back and forth, so they hired what is called in the drug game a "mule." They couldn't recruit mules directly from the Salerno family because those guys already had responsibilities, and they couldn't afford to be unavailable on the road for large chunks of time.

Most importantly, the risk of a mule getting arrested while on the road meant the Salerno family didn't want their mules to be traced back to them. They needed independent mule contractors. Therefore, they recruited young guys from the neighborhood, but we all learned hauling drugs didn't come without a set of headaches.

CARLO: Why do you guys keep hiring new mules?

SCHNAZE: We are on our fourth mule in as many months. I'll tell you what happened to the first three we shit-canned. For the first mule, I bought a new 2010 Lincoln Town car for $53,000. The car was beautiful with a light blue exterior and had every available option. The dark blue leather interior was like butter.

It was a nice car and would glide down the road like you were sitting in a spaceship. The trunk was huge enough for three or four people to be able to climb into it and lay down comfortably. The car was perfect for hauling a lot of drugs.

Everything began easy enough. The mule drove back and forth to Miami and took flights back and forth to deliver the money without a hitch. Then, one morning, I received a call from him. He was charged with a DUI and sat in a county jail in Mobile, Alabama.

He had fallen asleep at the wheel and drove the car through a corn field landing in a ditch, front end first. He was still asleep in the morning when the cops found him.

They impounded the car.

The mule expected me to drop everything and come get him. He said he felt horrible about it.

His bail was $1,500 and he needed another $450 to get the car released from being impounded.

Needless to say, I was fuming at this point. After I had the chance to settle down, I feared going to pick up the car because there was over 500 pounds of weed and cocaine in the trunk.

What if the cops checked it?

Worse yet, what if the trunk popped open at some point while the car was being towed?

On top of this, I had stupidly registered the car in my name. It all added up to I could be in jail like my mule.

Before I left New York on the flight to Alabama, I left instructions and money with Lucky. I warned him I may be calling that night from jail.

Most importantly, I told him he couldn't tell anyone in New York where I was because I had just told Johnny about the mule I hired, and he was proud of me for starting to build our own crew.

I couldn't afford for word to get back to Johnny that things were screwed up.

At the police department in Mobile, I paid my guy's bail, and I was fully prepared for the cop to ask for my driver's license, and walk from behind the counter to put his handcuffs on me.

Yet nothing happened.

We headed to where the car was impounded. I worried the cops would arrest me there. Yet again nothing happened.

I saw the car with its flat front tires, bent rims and front end screwed up. The car wasn't built to be a 4 X 4.

When I realized no one had discovered what was in the trunk, I had trouble holding back my enthusiasm.

For a screw up like this, anyone else in the Salerno family would have ordered a beating on this guy, but I just fired him. Beating him up wouldn't bring my car back or fix the situation. The way I saw it, the whole situation was my fault.

LUCKY: From that guy, we learned to do a better job with who we picked to be our next mule. Nevertheless, before we became better at it, we kept making hiring mistakes. The second mule was another young kid from the neighborhood.

He was flawless doing the drive to and from Miami. He loved driving the new car we bought him, which was the second new car we bought in as many months.

On his eighth run to Miami, he hit a snag.

For his flight to deliver the money to our Columbian, he checked the money bag as baggage and the airline misrouted the bag to Dallas instead of Miami.

He called to describe what happened.

I yelled at him, "You put $150,000 in cash in your bag, and you checked it?!"

The airline told him the bag would be put on the first flight from Dallas to Miami the following morning.

I punched the wall as hard as I could in anger.

I asked him, "Did you ever consider the possibility the Feds may be on to you?"

I couldn't believe he asked, "How is that possible?"

I had to enlighten him that the Feds do random luggage checks for drugs or large amounts of cash.

The Feds may have been delaying his bag so they could get DEA agents to the airport to apprehend him when he tried to pick up his bag the following morning.

He apologized, and I asked him where he was planning to stay for the night.

He answered, "The trip was supposed to be same day, there and back. I only brought $20 for food at the airport."

I was seething when I told him, "Stay at the airport. I'm flying down. I will call you when I land."

I arrived in Miami late that night and brought $30,000 in cash for bail and a lawyer in case he and/or I were arrested. Adding to my stress was I spoke with the Colombian the previous morning letting him know the drugs were sold on the latest shipment and the money was on its way to him.

Therefore, the money was no longer mine.

The money belonged to the Colombian.

Moreover, I didn't have extra cash available to cover the $150,000 if it was lost or my guy was arrested! This would be a big problem, and if I asked to delay the payment at this point, it wouldn't fly.

We went to the airport early the next morning. I stood a couple hundred yards away and observed everything for a long while. I was relieved when my guy walked up to the lost luggage counter agent, and she handed him the bag with no problem.

On the flight back to New York, I dug a little deeper and asked my guy why he checked the bag in the first place.

He explained, "I thought the money would be safer if I checked it."

This didn't make any sense to me.

I pressed him further on his answer, and he admitted another blunder on the trip before this one that he hadn't told me about.

On that trip, he almost lost the bag of money when he left it under a table at an airport burger joint before the flight.

CARLO: A burger joint?

LUCKY: Yeah, that bag had $180,000 in cash in it for anyone to grab. Fortunately, after he got on the plane, he begged the stewardess to let him off the plane to retrieve his bag. Fortunate for him, the bag was still where he left it.

SCHNAZE: We fired him too. Young mules are too immature and make too many mistakes. For the third mule, we chose someone older, but we forgot to check the most basic qualification to be a mule.

When he got locked up outside of Atlanta, Georgia in East Point County, it was for not having his driver's license.

His license wasn't suspended or lost.

He didn't have one!

This didn't make any sense either because we had seen him driving around the neighborhood for years.

He adamantly defended not having his driver's license, "I never had one. I don't need one to drive a car. I started driving when I was 13. I didn't have one then, and I don't have one now."

Boy, did we feel dumb.

Just because we hired an older guy, we couldn't assume he would be better or smarter than the younger guys. By the time I flew down there, he already appeared before a judge and tried to get the $933 ticket fee waived, but the judge put him on a monthly payment plan of $100 per month until the ticket was paid off.

We got the car released, and we drove back to New York.

He promised me he would get his license.

I gave him another chance, and he went back to work.

A few weeks passed, and he called us again from Fulton County jail near Atlanta. He was caught driving without a license again.

Now I was enraged, "No license?! You told me you took the test a month ago! You lied to me?!"

He said, "I didn't lie to you. I did take the test, but I didn't tell you I failed it."

I washed my hands of him and gave him some advice when I told him, "The time you are going to spend in jail won't be wasted time. Don't think it will give me pleasure to see you suffer, because it won't. You're fired."

Then, I hung up, went down there, picked up my car; and drove it back to New York without him. He did 68 days in Fulton County Jail.

The day he was released, he walked outside the jail, and there waiting for him was a cop from East Point County, Georgia.

The cop re-arrested him for an unpaid balance of $33 from his first ticket of driving without a license.

The original balance on that ticket was $933, but he only paid $900 of it, and thought "fuck it" for the last $33.

East Point County issued a warrant for his arrest for the unpaid balance.

He did another 73 days in the jail for East Point County before he was released.

Somehow, he found his way back to New York.

We accepted responsibility for our part. We gave a guy without a driver's license $250,000 worth of drugs to drive across the country.

How stupid were we?

LUCKY: Hey, I have some good news.

We've been selling a lot of cocaine at Johnny's bar since we took over distribution there a couple weeks ago.

It is an "after-hours" club after 4am, which is where lots of connected guys hang out and strippers go after they get off work. Most of the other clubs close at 2am.

Yesterday morning at 5am, Johnny asked me to stand guard outside the bathroom door while he setup his lines of coke on the bathroom counter.

He doesn't like to be disturbed when he snorts his coke.

I used the bathroom after him to take a piss, and I noticed the walls had cardboard taped to them instead of drywall.

I gave a perplexed look at the walls, left the bathroom, and sat next to Johnny at his table.

I asked Johnny, "What is the deal with the walls in the bathroom? Are you doing a remodel?"

He answers with a laugh, "Ha! The guys go in there at night after hours and do lines on the bathroom counter.

They end up talking for hours about scores inside the bathroom.

Then, they get paranoid from all the cocaine and start ripping the drywall out looking for bugs from the cops!

They never find one.

These fucking jerkoffs tear out my walls all the time, and I have to replace them!"

While I sat with Johnny, he noticed an unconnected guy come into the bar.

The guy was a neighborhood cocaine addict, and one of my best customers.

Johnny snarled at me, "I don't like coke heads coming into my bar. They're not the type of people I want to attract. This is a place for respectable wiseguys. Sell it to him this once and chase him off."

I told him this guy goes to the bathroom before he comes to see me because just the thought of being close to sniffing cocaine causes levels of excitement in his brain which triggers his bowels to explode. I called it cocaine shits. This is because when our guys receive a kilo of cocaine, they cut it down by mixing it with two kilos of baby laxative.

The baby laxative has the same powder consistency as cocaine.

From an original kilo of cocaine, they have three kilos of diluted cocaine that they sell as regular cocaine.

The coke head thinks it's the cocaine that causes his shits, but it's the baby laxative.

Johnny scowled, "That's too much dilution. Tell the guys I only want to sell pure cocaine here. We don't need to be greedy and cut it down."

JEALOUSY

Like most teenagers, I started to act up, rebel and push the boundaries with authority figures. The problem was all of the authority figures in my life were professional criminals, and the rules they taught me to follow had consequences if I didn't follow them.

These consequences were very different from other teenagers whose parents might punish them with being grounded for a short time or take away their car keys for a week. The rules I lived under were non-negotiable, and I needed a couple good lessons to help drive this point home.

Both of the lessons involved my first experiences with women.

The first lesson had to do with some of my first expanded responsibilities that came after a while of working at Johnny's bar.

When Johnny would go on vacation, I was in charge of the bar. I opened and closed it, oversaw ordering of supplies, took the phone calls for gambling bets, sold drugs under the counter, and managed the cash. I was barely old enough to drive, but the bartender along with the waitresses, all of whom were in their late twenties, answered to me in the absence of Johnny.

There was this girl who came in the bar regularly late at night. I knew she dated Johnny a few times, but so did a lot of the women who came in the bar. She wasn't Johnny's girlfriend or anything.

I had some confidence at this point, and I asked her out on a few dates. We had some fun together, and that was it. A few weeks later, I was at a bar down the street from Johnny's when Schnaze sat next to me.

He said, "Johnny needs to see you."

I asked, "Do you know what this is about?"

He replied, "I don't know, but why don't you order a shot of tequila? I'll have one with you."

We had a shot.

Then Schnaze said, "Order one more, and then let's go."

Alarm bells went off in my head.

How many times in the past was I the messenger for Johnny going to get someone who needed to be taught a lesson?

Then, Schnaze and I shared a third shot and left.

Johnny's bar was shaped as a long rectangle with a narrow front and long walk inside to the rear exit of the bar.

What was peculiar on this day was the front door to the bar was propped open along with the rear exit door.

When I stood outside the bar on the sidewalk and looked inside, I could see straight through to the back courtyard with Flanagan seated under a tree at a table holding a glass of wine.

Schnaze said my meeting with Johnny was in the courtyard.

I couldn't spot Johnny anywhere as I stood in the bar entrance.

I walked through the front door, and, like they always do, I saw guys inside the bar playing cards at different tables.

I gave a wave at the bartender, and he waved back.

As I walked through the door at the back of the bar to the courtyard, I felt a sudden punch to the right side of my stomach, and another punch landed on my face from the left side.

Immediately, I fell to the ground and curled up in a little ball as Johnny and Lucky kicked me furiously in the back, chest, stomach, legs, and head.

They both screamed at me.

September 16, 2010

JOHNNY: You low-life cocksucker!

LUCKY: You mother fucker!

JOHNNY: Take this!

LUCKY: I'm going to kill you!

JOHNNY: Don't you ever get involved with anybody in my personal life? Understood?

CARLO: Yeah, understood.

JOHNNY: OK, enough! Get up! Have a seat. You alright?

CARLO: I'm dizzy. My head is spinning.

JOHNNY: Give it a moment. Here is a few hundred dollars and my doctor's card.

CARLO: Thanks.

JOHNNY: Go see him this afternoon. Tell him I sent you. He'll see you right away. He is really good, the best. He'll get you fixed up. How are you feeling?

CARLO: I'm fucked up, but I'll be alright.

JOHNNY: Do you want a drink? Have a drink with me.

End of conversation dated September 16, 2010

Never again, did I talk to any woman Johnny did.

But there was one more lesson about women I had to learn.

This involved a girl I dated my age. It was nothing serious. We smoked weed together, but the problem was her older sister dated Johnny.

Johnny found out and told me, "Don't ever let me catch you seeing that girl or so help you God."

I did as he ordered. I avoided the girl, but she kept calling me and asking to get together. One night, I acquiesced and clandestinely brought her to a nice lookout near the Brooklyn Bridge.

We got high, messed around, and had a great time. I told her not to mention us to anyone, especially her sister.

The next day Johnny saw me in the bar, walked behind me, grabbed a margarita blender off the edge of the bar, and smacked it against the back of my head.

Blood was squirting everywhere from a gash in the back of my head. I hunched over and asked him, "What was that for?"

Johnny declared, "Don't ever blow off something I tell you. I'm teaching you a lesson. Now get out of here."

Lucky threw me out on to 101st Avenue, but not before he stripped off all my clothes and locked the front door of the bar behind me.

There I was naked and embarrassed holding my aching head in the middle of the afternoon on a busy street in Queens.

Cars went by, and some honked.

Where could I go?

I curled up in a ball and waited outside the door.

After 30 minutes, Lucky unlocked it.

Johnny sat down next to me at the bar, "Put on your clothes. Then, you need to go see my doctor again. But first, have a drink with me. Are you OK? You are doing great work. I'm sorry I had to do that. Stop making me do that. I hate it."

THE YOUNG BEAR

I knew a kid a couple years older than me who got involved in the drug game in a bold way while he was in high school. At 17 years old, he was a big dude with long, blond curly hair. He looked like a professional bodybuilder because he worked out all the time, used steroids and human growth hormone, and wore sleeveless shirts. He possessed a trigger temper and steel balls.

The Mexican cartel guys referred to him as "Oso", which means "bear" in Spanish. Some of the cartel guys called him "Oso Grande" which means, "Big Bear."

Oso dropped by the bar and talked about his background one afternoon.

> *November 9, 2010*
>
> CARLO: How did you get started in the drug game?
>
> OSO: A couple years ago, I was a junior in high school and it was close to the end of the school year. I did a current events report for one of my classes on the drug war. I read about how Mexico would develop into a supplier someday to challenge Colombia.
>
> This would make it much easier for drugs to come into the U.S. because the drugs could be driven across the Mexican-US Border rather than flying them from Colombia. Already, guys were getting rich doing it.
>
> I thought that there was no reason why I couldn't do this. I convinced myself to drive

down there to find a supplier. For my first potential customers, I had my entire high school.

To get permission to do the drive, I lived with my dad, I lied to my dad saying I was going for a week of camping with friends once summer break began. He believed it. He worked all the time and couldn't be bothered.

I drove my beat up car from Queens across the country to El Paso, Texas, and then across the border to San Juarez, Mexico. After a couple nights of trying to get to know the locals by going to bars and strip clubs.

I met some bartenders and dancers and asked around how could I get in touch with someone who could sell me marijuana.

One bartender put me in touch with a low level Mexican drug cartel representative. The rep said his people could get the drugs to Tucson and I could pick it up from there.

He warned me that the drive out of Arizona would be tough with cops as close as five miles apart looking for cars carrying drugs.

While I was in Mexico and before I left for the trip back home, I bought five pounds of weed for $1,500.

Once I arrived back in Queens, I figured I could unload it quickly for $5,000.

I hid the weed inside my car's passenger door, and attempted to cross the border.

The border guard asked me, "Why are you in San Juarez?"

I told him resolutely, "Sightseeing."

The guard wasn't convinced. He gave me a cynical look and pointed, "Yeah right, please pull your car over to section D."

Section D was where they tore apart cars looking for drugs.

They went through every corner of the car and found nothing.

I know how to hide shit.

From that trip, I built a multi-million-dollar business in my first year. Eventually, I hired smart kids from my high school as mules to drive the drugs from Tucson to the east coast. I developed routes for them not used by the other drug traffickers.

I became increasingly sophisticated with my routes taken by heading north or west before going east.

Also, I did car switches in garages near the borders of each state in order to have in-state plates.

Since I bought direct from the Mexican cartels, my costs were significant lower than other local dealers who bought from distributors who bought from other distributors.

Each distributor took a cut and the other dealers couldn't compete with me due to their higher costs.

Eventually, it made sense for the other dealers to become my customers.

Their increased business allowed me to negotiate better costs from the cartel. As my business grew, I became an important customer to them, and the cartel introduced me to its higher level members. Ultimately, I worked my way up to the son of the cartel boss who is the second in command. He is a lawyer and gay, not like I have a problem with that. What he does privately is his business as long as it doesn't involve me. His nickname is "The Prince."

I buy my weed by the truckload, and the loads are broken down into cars for travel, then sold in 15 pound blocks to distributors, who sell it to others in single pounds, who sell it to others in one ounce bags to the end users.

Each guy in the chain makes a few hundred dollars on each pound they sell.

I make the most at $600 per pound profit.

I learned to make distributors prepay for orders to avoid problems.

At all costs, I avoid putting myself in a situation where other drug dealers owe me money or where I sell drugs to the people who actually smoke it.

After a while, The Prince trusted me enough to invite me on a trip to see how the drugs came across the border.

At sunrise in the Arizona desert near the Rio Grande valley, we rode in a custom dune buggy with a chromed out racing engine like what you would see at a racetrack.

The buggy lights stayed off during the drive as we barreled through the desert at 100 miles per hour launching a dust cloud 50 feet high behind us.

I saw the Prince press a navigation system start button that had a precise location 10 miles away on it.

He listened intently to a walkie-talkie close to his ear.

Due to the rains that occur in the spring, the Rio Grande river swells.

To avoid being flooded, the U.S. border guard locations move away from the swelling river every few weeks.

When they move, the guards temporarily don't watch the border.

On the Mexico side of the river, the cartel guys watch for when the border guards move from their locations, and signals via walkie-talkies to groups of men near the river with back packs full of drugs and laying stomach down who slowly jog to the river bank where tree branches cover boats with paddles.

Once they are across, they load their backpacks into custom SUVs with elevated suspensions and oversized tires built for navigating the desert. After they clear the desert, the SUVs head to Tucson.

The cartel has another way of getting drugs across the border besides swimming across the river.

They pack vehicles with drugs and have mules drive it across through border towns.

The way the cartel deals with recruiting these mules is ruthless.

They recruit guys who are not smart enough to fight their way out of a paper bag. For example, they recruit young homeless guys from Hollywood Boulevard in Los Angeles by offering them a job driving a car.

What does the homeless guy have to lose? Of course he takes the job, he is homeless!

The cartel frames the homeless guy. He gets busted driving a car across the border loaded with drugs. The cops label him a major drug trafficker and drug kingpin.

The cops hold a press conference to celebrate the arrest.

The homeless guy faces life in prison and is now entangled in a high profile drug case of a U.S. citizen living in Mexico.

Would the public believe the homeless guy is a drug kingpin?

If the public saw an interview with him, it would be obvious he isn't. However, the public only sees his mug shot on the evening news.

The mirage is the public sleeps better at night thinking their government is protecting them. What a crock of shit.

I hear the jails in the U.S. are full of these idiots.

You may wonder, "Why does the cartel frame their own mules? It doesn't make any sense."

It does make sense. These mules keep up appearances that the drug war is being won when, in reality, the government hasn't won anything. The cartel keeps getting bigger and bigger, and the war is just being manipulated.

There is an unlimited supply of these homeless guys. The cartel has a name for them. They call them, "crash test dummies."

These dummies serve as sacrificial lambs for law enforcement both in Mexico and the United States. When it is time for a sacrificial lamb, the cartel packs the car with drugs so poorly that the border dogs can smell it from a mile away.

The dummies never physically see or know who they really deal with from the cartel. For example, a voice on a phone orders a dummy to pick up a car and go to this or that place.

The cartel jam packs the car with drugs hidden in the seat cushions, trunk and doors, inside the tire rubber, and gas tank. Then, they leave the keys in the ignition, lock it in a garage, and give the address to the dummy of where to pick the car up in Mexico and where to drive it in the U.S. The cartel communicates with their dummies using fake names on disposable phones that are thrown away after one use.

The guys the dummies are set up to work with down in Mexico are also crash test dummies. When one dummy gets arrested, the cartel expects him to rat on the others in his group to avoid a life sentence and instead get five years.

Once the dummy identifies all the others, the evidence trail ends, and the government declares, "We have won another victory in the war on drugs!"

In the government's desperate rush to declare each victory, it never really takes the time to discover who they just arrested is a crash test dummy. I don't think they care. It's a joke.

I heard about a prime example of a dummy called "Rabbit." He looked like he could be a doctor or a lawyer, but he was dumb as rocks and mentally handicapped.

When he was in unpleasant situations, he had meltdowns where he yelled loudly. He belonged in a mental institution. Most would call him a society misfit. However, when he wasn't having a meltdown, he has a heart of gold. He would do anything for anybody.

The cartel recruited him off the streets in San Diego and brought him to Tijuana as a mule. They gave him a three-bedroom house, a new BMW convertible, and a ready-made family: a wife, three adult kids and two grandchildren. He had never known such a life.

He told a friend of mine about his new family, "She loves me. I call her children my children. They call me dad. Those are my grandchildren.

When I was recruited to be a mule, I was unemployed, hungry, and scared. For the first time in my life, I learned what it was like to be loved, and be a part of a family.

I finally have a normal life. I take my family to the store, and I pay for what they need. We go out to dinner together. We watch movies together. The happiness I feel with them is more than I felt over my prior 28 years of life. Do you understand?"

Rabbit used to sing to his "daughter's" stomach when she was pregnant with his "granddaughter." He was there when the baby was born. He would boast how he was the first person the baby saw in this world. He believed he may not be related by blood, but he saw himself as the baby's grandfather.

Rabbit lived his dream life in Tijuana for only 10 months before he was arrested.

My friend tried to talk some sense into Rabbit when he spoke to him when he was locked up, "You are not married to the woman you call your wife. I don't want to sound cold, but did you ever think that she was provided to you by the cartel? Has she crossed the border to visit you since you have been incarcerated?"

Rabbit made excuses for her, "She can't leave Mexico, but I know she loves me."

Then, Rabbit asked cluelessly, "Why is the government being so hard on me? I didn't know what was in the car, doesn't that matter? I am just a mule, a glorified truck driver. All I did was drive stuff across the border."

My friend answered, "Ignorance is not an excuse. You were caught transporting a lot of drugs across the border, over 50 pounds of meth and a 100 kilos of cocaine.

Do you recognize that what you did was a crime?"

My friend tried being straight with him.

Either way, whether Rabbit cooperated or not, the fact was he would never see his "family" again.

A few weeks later, the woman he called his wife would be redeployed by the cartel to be with another mule like him.

I have a chemist friend who taught me how to manufacture meth without risking blowing up half of a building.

It sells for $400-600 for an eight ball, 3.5 grams, and only costs about $40 to make, which is 10 times the initial investment.

Meth makers buy about $600-1000 in breathing filters, scales, and select chemicals to setup shop.

There was an idiot last month in Washington Heights who blew up his entire kitchen, dining room, and half the apartment upstairs making his meth bullshit.

He lost four fingers on his right hand, and he only had a thumb left.

I am not sure if he will regain sight out of his right eye.

Luckily, no one was home upstairs.

Meth makers are not only to themselves, but their immediate neighbors.

In other areas of the country, these meth labs show up in remote locations where an explosion only destroys the trailer home they are usually setup in, but here in the Northeast, there are too many people packed into a city block.

I thought about selling it. I bought all the lab equipment online to manufacture it.

However, on top of the safety concerns, meth dealers get slammed by the Feds.

You can get locked up for 10 years for an eight ball. 3.5 grams is a tiny amount for 10 years of your life.

It didn't seem worth it.

For me, it made no sense.

Besides recruiting homeless guys, the cartel finds plenty of other guys who possess what I call a "self-destructive streak."

They are young and seek adventure. They risk everything when it isn't necessary. They erroneously see themselves as having nothing to lose.

The tragic thing is they are prepared to risk up to 20 years in jail for as little as $5,000 in cash during an afternoon drive across the border!

Back to my business.

Within six months of building it, I dropped out of high school and moved out of my dad's place.

As long as I drop by my dad's place once a week when he is home, he doesn't have a problem with me living out on my own.

He is into weed, and I drop off a bunch at his place when I visit.

I moved to an apartment on the Upper East Side of Manhattan.

Initially, my landlord hesitated renting to me.

My young age concerned him.

When I offered him two years of rent in cash upfront, his eyes nearly popped out of his head. In addition, I offered to pay cash for two parking spaces.

I needed them for my new black Lexus and new Infiniti SUV. I paid cash for the cars too.

When I first moved there, I threw parties right out of a huge college fraternity, but none of us ever went to college, and the whores we had over at these parties could never get into college.

During the parties, couples occupied the bedrooms and bathrooms, so other couples hooked up in one corner of the living room while a card game was being played on the other side of the room.

It was like a construction site, where three guys watch and one guy does the work, except that the one guy working wasn't working, he was having sex.

The guys playing cards would cheer on the guy having sex or would look over and taunt him by saying, "I need a break from my game! When you are done with her, let me have a turn. I'll be quick!"

End of conversation dated November 9, 2010

Given all the problems Schnaze and Lucky had with their mules, it was easy to convince them to switch to Oso as their drug supplier.

JENNIFER

I met a girl named Jennifer Melendez at a Manhattan club. She was a couple years older than me, a real knockout, beautiful. She had long, straight black hair, dark brown eyes, attractive facial features, high cheekbones, and a petite 5'6" body with a thin athletic build. She wore tight jeans with a form fitting top to show off her curves. She was Puerto Rican and grew up in the Bronx.

I made sure Johnny never met her.

I talked to her a few times before I had a dream about her. My eyes opened wide as I stared at the ceiling. She floated above me like a graceful angel dressed in white satin.

Her eyes sparkled and her lips gently smiled.

I imagined her as the first woman to come along and take a genuine interest in me.

I felt real love radiate from her.

With her, I felt self-confident, safe and secure.

I asked her out on a date at my place. I planned to make a nice Italian dinner called Broccoli Raab from scratch. It had a red sauce with sausages and meats, seasoning, broccoli, and angel hair pasta.

To help set the mood, I would play my favorite Frank Sinatra songs. For dessert, I planned to make a raspberry cheesecake.

I asked her to dress up for the dinner, and then I would take her out to Manhattan clubs afterwards.

The elevator made a beeping sound as I stepped out and pulled out my keys to unlock the door. Three young punks with guns ran up behind me yelling obscenities and pushed me inside my condo on the floor.

One of them stomped my shoulder with the heel of his black leather boot, while another wrapped duck tape over my mouth. The other one walked around the apartment looking for money.

This was the first time someone robbed me.

One of the punks told me, "Look at me, you cock sucker! You are going to tell us where the drugs and money are, understood?

If we find that you lied to us about a single dollar, bag of weed or pill anywhere in this apartment, I am going to walk to your kitchen drawer, grab the biggest fork, and stick it in your eye!"

I snapped back, "If you are all such tough guys, then why are you wearing masks?

Is it because you're afraid I will recognize you?"

He yelled, "You piece of shit. Tell me where the money is!"

They smacked me around for 30 seconds before I gave them what they wanted and told them, "You pieces of shit.

Check inside the freezer in a plastic sherbet half-gallon container. It is full of $100 bills. It is yours. Take it and leave."

One of them shouted, "What a score!"

I had no idea my date Jennifer heard the commotion from outside and kicked open the front door. She held a pistol aimed at the young punks and screamed, "Throw your guns on the floor! Let me ask you all a question. Should I have you put in a trunk and dropped off at the local salvage yard?"

Then, she shot one in the leg. He bellowed, "You shot me! You bitch!"

She declared, "This is Ozone Park! No matter how loud you yell, nobody is going to call the police. Especially not about any noises coming from this place. Get on the fucking floor or I will blow your fucking head off, mother fucker! Lay on the ground with your arms out! Now listen to me. Do any of you need to have your diaper changed?

The three of you look like you are capable of having a good head on your shoulders, and I need you to concentrate on what I am about to tell you, understood? I am going to report to a few stone cold killers that if anything happens to my man or I in the future, then all three of you will be tortured and then executed, understood?

Leave your wallets on the kitchen island, along with everything in your pockets, understood?

And take off those silly masks. I want to look into your eyes. Now hobble your sorry asses out of my man's home, and do not ever let me see you again."

They left.

Jennifer immediately asked, "Are you OK? How is my makeup?"

I queried, "You carry a pistol to a date? You look beautiful."

She answered, "Like I said, this is Ozone Park. You never know what kind of hoodlums are lurking around. You still cooking for us?"

We had a great time that night.

After a few months, we were an item. When I wasn't working, Jennifer and I were fucking.

Sometimes her blond, busty, tall, and unfortunately, lesbian roommate would join in. Her name was Heidi. I'm not joking.

Heidi had a crush on Jennifer, but Heidi hated me and any other guy.

Heidi liked to watch Jennifer get fucked.

When Heidi got turned on, she would let me do coke lines off her belly and suck her huge natural tits, while she caressed Jennifer.

One time, I got Heidi wasted and fucked her after Jennifer.

But the next morning when Heidi found out we did it, she practically kicked my ass.

It was great.

TEST & REWARD

Johnny walked over confidently, and asked me to join him in the back room of the bar. It was a secretive room with linoleum floors, different from the tile and grout floors in the rest of the bar.

This room was where Johnny conducted real business and the linoleum floors cleaned up easily.

I had only seen inside the room through a cracked door when someone important walked inside or out. I had never been inside.

I asked Johnny, "Did I mess something up? Did I not do something quick enough? Did I not get enough money? I don't belong in this room. Why me? I am nobody."

Johnny reassured me, "I need a small favor from you. You will be sending a message from me. I need you to pay a visit to a guy's address, create a mess with what he has in the basement garage, and leave. Can you do that for me?"

I accepted the job and visited the garage when the guy wasn't home. The garage appeared like a professional mechanic shop with eight classic cars restored to flawless, mint condition. When I turned on the fluorescent light, the chrome and paint on the cars sparkled like they just rolled off the factory floor over 30 years ago.

I hesitated and thought, "What a shame to mess up these cars."

But I did as Johnny instructed. I turned the garage into a demolition derby at a county fair.

A couple days later, I hung out at a nearby park with young guys from the Salerno family, most of whom were older than me. A large, black Cadillac Fleetwood, the biggest Cadillac they make, pulled up slowly 20 yards away, and the rear window rolled down. Johnny was in the back seat. He pointed at me and waved me over to the car.

At the time, I thought, "Why is he calling me out in front of everybody?"

The minute I approached, Johnny praised me, "You did a real nice job with that thing I asked you to do. You have a girlfriend?"

I answered, "I have a girl I like a lot."

Then, Johnny gave me an exclusive invite, "This Saturday, you ask this girl out to the Ada Romona restaurant.

Ask to see the head host.

Tell him you are there to sit at my table in the back. Order and drink whatever you want on the menu.

Tell him to put it on my tab. Stay as long as you want. It's on me."

I thanked him. This restaurant and his table in the back were well known in Queens and Brooklyn as Johnny's hangout. The restaurant was where the top wiseguys from many families hung out.

Nobody could sit at Johnny's table unless Johnny allowed it. This was like being invited to the White House while the President was away and eating at his table.

Even though Johnny was a Captain in the Salerno Family and he had two levels of bosses above him, the other bosses regarded him as the future of the family.

It was a matter of time before he would be the boss of all bosses.

For the date, I wore my best suit, and she wore a tight classy black dress. I strolled up to the head host and self-assuredly asked, "How are you doing? We are here for the table in the back."

I pointed to Johnny's table and the host nervously looked over.

The host requested clarification, "You want to sit at that table?"

Again, I said, "Yes, that one."

He countered in a weak voice, "Are you sure you mean that one?"

There was an awkward pause before I said, "Yes, that one, if you need to, you can call him."

The host backed down, "No, that won't be necessary, please follow me."

As my girl and I were lead to the table, people in the restaurant at different tables coyly looked up, tried to subdue their curious amazement, and attempted to determine if I was somebody important.

In the backs of their minds, they thought if they didn't know me, then they probably should.

We ordered everything on the menu, and drank a lot of wine.

I wanted to make a big impression on Jennifer, and I think I did. I looked like a young guy putting things together.

Despite the fact I was fifteen years old, I thought and lived like an adult. She was eighteen.

December 15, 2010

CARLO: I don't like dating a lot of different girls. I want a serious relationship.

JENNIFER: When I originally met you, I didn't think you were looking for a relationship, why me?

CARLO: I have to admit, at first, it was physical. I like petite brunettes. I like the fire in a Latin woman. And you?

JENNIFER: I could sense you had a soft, romantic heart. That is what attracted me. I tend to be attracted to Italian or Latin guys. However, with you, you are Italian, but you have blue eyes and light hair.

CARLO: I never opened myself up to a woman or wanted to open myself up. I felt I could do that with you, from the moment we met. Chemistry, I guess.

JENNIFER: Why couldn't you open up with anyone else?

CARLO: I felt abandoned by anyone I relied on or loved, like no one wanted me. I learned to rely on myself, and never be vulnerable.

JENNIFER: That is so sad. When it comes to a relationship, what do you want?

CARLO: To have a good time together, to laugh with one another, to appreciate each other, to protect each other, to treasure what we have, to be good to each other always. If something hurts the other person, I want it to hurt me too.

I want someone where we can be 100 years old together, you understand? What do you want?

JENNIFER: I want no fantasyland, no trying to be more than we are. I want to be the only person he wants. With each other, we let our walls down, and open our hearts. I want to be enough for the other person. I want to wake up beside him in the morning, every morning. I want him to fight to have or keep me. It scares me that wanting a life with a man and just being happy, won't be enough for him, and he won't be content. We could build our dream together one step at a time.

CARLO: Inside of me there is much bitterness, but with you I find patience.

JENNIFER: I really do that much for you?

CARLO: Lately, all I can think about is you. I am restless, but with you I find peace.

MAURICE FROM EAST BROOKLYN

Maurice became the biggest weed dealer in Brooklyn and Oso supplied him. Maurice dealt from five different apartments in his 100+ unit building. The coming and going of people never raised any red flags with the DEA or others.

Maurice watched everything from his 20th floor apartment staring at the Verrazano Bridge in the distance. Maurice used to boast, "You are safer here than anywhere else in New York City. I have every cop in my neighborhood paid off. Ain't nobody going to bother you. You can drive right up."

He was right.

His guys watched for cars, and waived them in the apartment building underground garage like they were VIPs.

A deal could take as little as 20 seconds.

Hand them the money and drive away with the merchandise.

In addition to drug dealing, Maurice ran a bouncer service for clubs in Manhattan. At the time, his service hired the best dressed, professional bunch of big and tall guys.

The three of us met at a restaurant near Oso's place in Central Park called Tavern on the Green. It was a cool spring day and our outside table had views of the horse carriages prancing along 75 yards away.

Maurice wore a dark blue suit and a black hat. He could have been mistaken for a banker or stock trader, except for the two-inch scar from an AK-47 bullet that ran below his left eye.

CARLO: Nice to meet you. How are you doing?

MAURICE: It isn't easy being sleazy. If I ain't making it, I'm faking it. Let's do some mental hygiene and wash our brains with this fine liquor.

A toast to life and new friends. I have a saying and it goes like this, "You know we have to be ready, so we don't have to get ready, because we are already ready." You dig? Cheers, let's converse and escape. I, myself and me, we all agree.

Don't believe the history books. I'm fittin' to tell you something about every war. All wars are fought over opium. Opium makes heroin, the most valuable commodity in the world.

You may think, what about the American Revolutionary war? I'll tell you about that. The British used to take opium grown here and sell it to the Chinese. The British used to tax the shit out of it. Too much taxation without representation of our opium. We said enough of that bullshit and had the Boston Tea Party.

You may also think, what about the Civil War? I'll tell you about that too. Believe me when I say that slaves picked fields of opium growing all over the South! Many Americans died fighting over that shit.

How about more recent wars like Viet Nam or the Middle East? These are an open and shut cases. We all know that these countries are right next to a bunch of countries that fuck with opium.

I have to tell you that the Middle East wars weren't over oil as everyone thinks. No. Where are the largest opium fields in the world? Afghanistan. What country is next to Afghanistan? Iraq.

It's all a drug conspiracy to pull the wool over our eyes.

OSO: OK, you are right Maurice.

MAURICE: Don't patronize me. I'm being real.

OSO: I know. Can we switch from your history lesson to a different topic?

MAURICE: Shoot.

OSO: The people who go to clubs, they are looking to have a good time and fun night out. Right?

MAURICE: Yeah sure.

OSO: There are plenty of drinks, booze, wine beer, dancing, music, girls, guys everywhere, right? Here is my question, do they ask your bouncers where they can buy weed?

MAURICE: All the time, people be asking, it's crazy.

CARLO: I want to discuss a business opportunity with your bouncer service and tying that into Carlo's club connections via the Salerno family. How about we try selling $20 hydro bags together? I could supply your guys.

MAURICE: What is hydro? How much does a $20 bag have in it?

CARLO: Hydro is Hydroponic Weed grown in greenhouses in Canada. It is the best weed out there, lots of THC in it, and the stuff gets people high. Each bag has about four joints in it.

MAURICE: How much do my guys make for selling each bag?

CARLO: On a $20 bag, you can earn $7 a bag and split it with your guys, however you want.

(Maurice pauses and thinks).

MAURICE: When can we try it out?

MY BIG BROTHER AL

Alfonso (Al) Toracio is the only child of Johnny Toracio. His parents divorced when Al was a baby. Soon thereafter, Al's mother remarried another wiseguy who was from a Long Island family. This meant that both Al's father and stepfather, his male role models, were wiseguys growing up. Al was 10 years older than me and I heard the stories about him. I was the closest thing he had to a brother, but due to our age difference, the fact that he lived in Long Island, and I lived 45 minutes away in Queens, we didn't see each other very much or relate well with one another.

Al became involved in the criminal lifestyle early like me; however, he wasn't encouraged into it by his father or stepfather. They were all adamantly against it. The more they encouraged him to do well in school, play sports, and prepare for college, the more he rebelled and cut classes to hang out with the neighborhood tough guys. At the time, there was no way to break through to Al. His mind was made up. He was going to be not only a mobster, but the best mobster, in the way he saw a mobster could be. I think deep down he was competitive with his father and stepfather and he was going to go further and faster up the mob hierarchy than they could imagine. What Al lacked in intelligence, he made up for in drive and determination.

Whereas I chose to learn the gambling business and later the weed business, Al chose a more traditional path to rising up the mob ranks through violence. Without anyone's knowledge, he did his first hit when he was just 16. This wasn't just any ordinary "hit", it was a hit on a connected guy who was suspected of being an informant for the Feds. The guy was twice as old as Al and pretty tough in his own right. Even so, early one morning Al waited outside the guy's townhouse, and shot him in cold blood on the street in the back of the head. Then, Al went home to watch the murder get covered on the local morning news shows.

When Al was 17, he began shaking down local businesses. The first time Al shook down a restaurant he walked in like the place was his, and asked for the owner. He promptly walked the owner to the back alley outside. The owner was about six inches taller than Al and weighed 300 pounds.

April 25, 2011

Owner: What do you want kid?

Al: I'm here to protect you and your place.

Owner: What are you talking about? You aren't even done with puberty you can't protect me. Scram kid.

Al: I'm not going anywhere.

Owner: I'm about to call the police. Stop joking around.

Al: This is no joke.

Owner: Go fuck off!

Al: You're going to start paying me!

Owner: You won't get a dime from me. You little shit!

Al: Get in the blue dumpster in the alley. Get in right now or I pull the trigger!

Owner: You are going to regret this.

End of conversation dated April 25, 2011

With the owner being so heavy, it took him a couple tries before he could climb into the dumpster and plop himself on top of the old smelly kitchen scraps and fermenting garbage. The owner went from a defiant look on his face to now having a worried one. When Al slid the top of the dumpster closed, and jammed the top closed with a stick he found nearby, the owner was scared for his life.

Inside the dumpster was pitch black. Outside, Al took three steps back, aimed the gun a few feet to the left from where the owner climbed in, and fired a bullet. Pop! Inside, near the owner's feet, a small ray of light came in from the hole created by the bullet. The owner started screaming. Pop! Pop! Pop! Three more new rays of light inside the dumpster were closer to where he sat. The owner yelled out he'd pay whatever Al wanted. Then Al let him out. Once word spread in the neighborhood about Al, everybody got in line to pay.

While other kids Al's age learned how to drive a car, date girls, do homework, and get ready for whatever their plans would be after high school, Al was developing a reputation as a feared mobster. Al was different from his father in that Johnny was respected and smart to go along with being able to solve problems without a gun. Al was respected only because he was feared. No one ever wanted to be caught in the room when Al got pissed off, because no one could predict how violent he would get. As Al got older, he got worse.

Al earned his button when he was 21. He had his own crew made up of guys who were young and aggressive like him. By the time he was 25, Al was a Captain in the Salerno family. He was the youngest Captain ever in its history. The young guys coming up all idolized him. Johnny was hesitant about fully endorsing Al because he believed a candle that burns twice as bright only lasts half as long. I agreed with him. We had seen too many guys with violent beginnings meet violent ends, and this happened sooner than anyone anticipated.

On top of all this, Al had an ego. He needed to show off whatever power and money he had to others. This included dressing in the most expensive suits, wearing the best jewelry, driving the best cars, and living in the best houses.

When he went out, he always had to have the biggest roll of $100 bills in his pocket, go the best restaurants, gamble at the best casinos, date the prettiest girls. On the job, he liked to give orders to a guy in front of others, and if a guy needed to be punished, he preferred to do it publicly. Al was the type of guy where if he ever became the top boss of the Salerno family, he would look forward to watching news stories about himself.

Al could be guilty of overextending himself and his crew on a potential score. A good example of this is when Al read an article online about a young billionaire banker named Conrad Edwards who was a workaholic and spent a lot of his time at his office in Greenwich, CT.

Al had the idea to kidnap Mr. Edwards and extort him for $5 million.

This would be Al's largest potential score he had done so far in his criminal career.

Al watched Mr. Edwards for several weeks before he developed his plan. He noticed that Mr. Edwards worked late almost every night during the week. Al decided to kidnap him as he left his office. Then, tie him up, throw him in a trunk, and go to a safe house nearby.

Al could threaten Mr. Edwards that if he didn't go to his bank in the morning to wire $5 million to an overseas account, it would be over for him.

Once the wire was received overseas, then Al could wire it a few more times to several other accounts in other names, withdraw the money and have it laundered back to the states. Al planned this all on his own like he did a lot of his early scores.

When I heard about the plan afterwards I thought, "Why kidnap the guy after work the night before? Why not kidnap him on the way to work and then go right to the bank?" That way, there would be less time for the score to get screwed up.

The night started off going as planned with Al driving to Greenwich.

He parked the car and hid in a set of bushes near the front office door out of view of security cameras.

Then, he grabbed Edwards as he walked out the door, blindfolded him, stuffed a rag in his mouth, tied his hands behind his back and his feet together, took his cell phone and wallet, carried him to the car, threw him in the trunk, and drove to a safe house 10 minutes away.

They sat him in the living room, and Al laid out the terms for what needed to happen in the morning.

Edwards agreed, they turned on a baseball game on TV for a couple hours.

They started to become comfortable around each other and began making small talk.

May 10, 2011

Al: I am hungry. I haven't eaten all day. I didn't see any places driving over here. It's 10 pm, who's open this late anyway? Fast food is probably open, but I want a good meal from a restaurant. We are in the middle of nowhere. My cell phone barely gets reception here.

Edwards: Excuse me, if you don't mind me making a suggestion?

Al: Go ahead.

Edwards: Thank you, I know a number of great restaurants in the area still open at this hour.

Al: What kind of restaurants?

Edwards: Italian, Chinese, seafood, steak, barbeque or burgers, you name it.

Al: Chinese sounds good. I like the sweet and sour chicken, on pork fried rice.

Edwards: This Chinese place is the best, five stars. They make everything fresh daily, even the fortune cookies. Their almond cookies are to die for. May I make a suggestion? You may want to consider calling in your order and have them deliver it to my office so you won't get lost.

Al: I don't know.

Edwards: I have an account at the Chinese place you can use. I order from there all the time. You are welcome to order whatever you want. They take only 20 minutes to deliver. No one knows I'm missing yet, least of which, the Chinese restaurant who would take your order. You'll have your money in the morning and be on your way.

Al: I could map it on my phone really quick. What's the name and address?

Edwards: I have it as a contact in my phone. The password to get in is 2008. 2008 was the year I met my wife and everything changed for me. She is the love of my life. Are you married?

Al: No, I won't be for a while. Have you been faithful to your wife for all these years?

Edwards: Yes, I never desired another woman after meeting her. I found my true love.

Al: That's special, I hope I find someone like that.

Edwards: Have faith. I believe for every man there is that special woman who will seize his heart, shake his senses, and satisfy his burning desires.

Al: You've given me hope I'll find someone someday.

Edwards: Be patient, love will come for you. It's inescapable. Name of the restaurant is Bobby Chang's. If you want to write down what you want, I could call the restaurant for us. By the time we get there, our orders should be ready. You could walk in and pick it up. Throw me in the trunk.

Al: Ok, let's watch the last inning of the game, order our food, and then leave.

End of conversation dated May 10, 2011

Al had the balls and the smarts to kidnap a billionaire and then have the guy give him life advice and buy him dinner. This was something rarely achieved by such a young gangster. However, the billionaire had smarts out of Al's or anybody else's league.

When they were on their way to the restaurant, they were passed by a cop car speeding at 80 miles per hour with his lights flashing.

This spooked Al initially, but he kept driving.

After a couple more minutes, another cop car passed them with his lights flashing, and this time, with his sirens blaring.

Then, another cop car passed.

Al was out of his mind.

Al was now a charter member of the long list of men who had been outsmarted by Mr. Edwards.

The billionaire tricked his kidnapper to input in his phone his personal emergency code of "2008," which was to be used if he was ever kidnapped or abducted.

The code sent alarm bells to his wife, his parents, his personal security, the local police, and FBI.

Mr. Edwards had a history of success, and this situation was no exception.

Al let Mr. Edwards out on the side of the road that night unharmed, and drove back to Queens.

Mr. Edwards hired two personal body guards to follow him at all times going forward.

THE BOSS

Johnny was a gangster 24 hours a day, 7 days a week. This meant he expected those around him to live the same way.

When it came to Johnny, the rules always applied to everybody else.

He knew all the moves on the street because he made his money off the streets. Johnny always got people to play the card he dealt.

Johnny used to correct me when I would try to be a tough guy.

He would say, "You aren't cut out to be a gangster, you are too smart for that. Learn the gambling, loansharking and drug sides of the business. That is where you belong. Use your head, any dummy can be violent."

On this day, I dropped by Johnny who welcomed me in his bar's basement lounge.

> *June 14, 2015*
>
> JOHNNY: There's my guy! Get in here!
>
> If we can't be on top in this jungle there is no reason to play the game! Everything is coming together for us. Get used to this life. Come do some rocks with me.
>
> CARLO: You knocked a few cocaine rocks on the floor. Do you want me to pick those up?
>
> JOHNNY: Forget about it. The coke whores will be down here later, and they vacuum the floor

with their noses looking for rocks like that. Enjoy yourself! Here, have some!

You want to hear a funny story? I had this mortician guy I know cutoff a dead man's prick, the whole kielbasa, balls and everything.

He put the prick in a jar filled with formaldehyde. This dead guy was hung like a horse and I needed one of those big jars.

I have my guys use the jar when they do collections on deadbeats that can't payoff their loans.

They show the jar and say, "pay me now or I'll take your prick like I did to this guy!"

All the color drains from the deadbeat's face.

Magically, any money owed to us suddenly appears.

That jar makes me a lot of money.

But wait, there's more. I have another tool like the jar that may help me make money too.

We found out one of our guys has a pet alligator named Godzilla.

He got it as a baby when it fit in a fish tank. He took good care of it, fed it the best food, lots of fresh chicken and beef.

The alligator outgrew the tank. He bought one of those big aquarium tanks.

He kept feeding it and it grew too big for that.

Godzilla is 6 feet long with long sharp teeth!

He can't buy a tank big enough, and he can't let it roam the house, so he keeps it in his basement.

The problem is Godzilla is driving his wife crazy!

She can't go down to the basement anymore and has to worry that the basement door is closed. Otherwise, Godzilla will take a bite out of her foot.

She gave her husband an ultimatum, "Godzilla needs to go!"

Tonight, Schnaze and Lucky Charms are picking it up.

I have a little visit they will make to a schmuck who owes me a lot of money.

They will threaten the schmuck with, "we haven't fed this alligator in three days, give us our money, or you can choose which hand gets fed to Godzilla!"

I am not sure yet if I should keep the alligator to use on other people. We'll see how the first encounter goes.

If it doesn't work out, then I'll have them drop the beast off in the Central Park reservoir. It's as big as a lake.

CARLO: That would make one hell of a nightly news story. Hey, how is Al doing?

JOHNNY: My son Al has problems with his probation officer. He met him for the first time yesterday.

His probation officer was agitated right off the bat saying, "I've read the details of your case. I know personally the FBI Agent Matera who completed your investigation.

Agent Matera told me directly, "Al is one of those criminals who pursues the most notorious crimes. His crimes come from a place of excess, unlike other criminals whose crimes may be driven by necessity."

The officer goes on scolding him, "I have to tell you. I have no idea how or why you only received five years of probation for your sentence. The FBI did their homework on you for years. By getting such a small sentence you invalidated their efforts to protect society from you."

What a jerk.

Al interrupted him and said, "Someone else confessed to most of the crimes I was charged with."

The officer jumped down his throat, "Save that bullshit for the judge and your sleazy lawyer. I know what kind of scumbag you are!

I was hand-picked to be your P.O.

I am going to watch you like a hawk, understand? Like a hawk!"

Al softly answered, "Ok, no problem."

The officer changed gears and asked, "What are your plans for employment?"

Al told him he planned to be a clerk at the Electrician's Union office.

The officer again jumped down his throat, "Bullshit! I know your family controls the union cards. Where else can you work?"

Al paused and then answered, "Costello's Waste Disposal in Queens."

The officer again shot back, "Bullshit! I know your family controls that too!"

Al meekly asked him, "What do you want me to do?"

The officer answered, "Find a job with no mob ties! There is a long list of stipulations that are contingent upon you remaining on probation, got it?

If I catch you hanging out with any of your mob low life's or going to a known mob establishment, you are going back to jail for five years, understood?

I believe you belong in jail, got it?

You are my number one priority case to watch.

I will be showing up unannounced at your job, your home, the places you used to hang out, the places you plan to hang out. I will be everywhere. I am on you.

You make me sick just looking at you. Get out
of here before I lock you up!"

CARLO: That is tough.

JOHNNY: You're telling me. Al needs to keep his
nose clean for a while.

THE TRAGIC HERO

June 17, 2015

JOHNNY: The Justice Department is hard on people, even good people.

Do you want to hear the most tragic story I heard from when I was locked up?

There was an Army veteran of the war in Afghanistan. He fought and killed many terrorists during his time there. He is an American hero.

He came back from his tour in the Middle East.

He was home for two weeks of leave with his family before heading to his next duty assignment.

He had been in the army for six years and was planning to be a soldier for his career.

CARLO: What happened?

JOHNNY: While home on leave, his sister called him one night crying hysterically.

Her husband was not a nice man. He was abusive to her. When he got mad, he hit her and threw her into walls.

I believe a man who hits a woman deserves the shit beat out of him. Don't you?

Well, this very evening when his sister called, her husband had kicked her in the back knocking her to the floor.

She was six months pregnant.

She didn't lose the baby.

The Army guy headed over to his sister's place, confronted her husband, and told him if he laid a hand on her again that will be the end of him.

Her husband said no one talks to him like that and took a swing at him.

The Army guy used his fighting skills and put the husband in the hospital for three months.

For the first 60 days of his hospital stay, the husband was in a coma.

He deserved it, right?

But the local police paid the Army guy a visit and questioned him about what happened.

The cop asked why he hurt his sister's husband so badly. He told the cop his honest answer, "I wanted to kill him."

This earned the Army guy an attempted murder charge that was downgraded in court to aggravated battery. The judge gave him three years in state prison.

His military career was over. He was dishonorably discharged.

He thought the military would defend him initially when the police arrested him given that he was a soldier and everything.

Can you believe it? An American hero defending his pregnant sister against a piece of shit husband.

And the American hero is the one who was punished severely.

He was turned into a second class citizen due to a momentary lapse of rational thinking where he let his anger take over.

CARLO: His story is tragic. I agree.

Do I believe his sister's husband needed the shit kicked out of him? Sure.

Do I believe a three-month hospital stay was the appropriate punishment? Why not?

HILLBILLY HEROIN

June 19, 2015

JOHNNY: Are you still staying away from drugs?

CARLO: I tried a little weed.

JOHNNY: Don't go beyond weed. Let me tell you something. I've seen drugs fuck up people's lives.

It is important to be careful with choosing where you buy your drugs.

Junkies are the worst. They will accept their drugs from anybody. Don't let yourself ever get to that point.

I've heard of scumbag drug dealers selling junkies roach killer and telling them its heroin, meth or PCP. Roach killer is cheap.

They call it "Hillbilly Heroin."

Let me tell you, it just isn't poisonous to roaches. That shit fucks your body up permanently.

The dealers make a big profit on it.

It is made like this.

A group of bikers are in the backyard of an older house on a secluded lot with dense trees. They are drinking beers and talking. One biker has the seat off of his motorcycle. He has battery cables running from the battery to a wire mesh screen. Another biker is spraying roach killer at a 45 degree angle on to the electrified, red hot screen.

As the roach killer hits the screen, it becomes a powder form and falls like tiny snowflakes from the screen to a metal pan below it.

The biker uses a razor blade to scrape up the powder and places it into a plastic bag to sell to his customers.

I'll tell you a story about what this crap can do to somebody. A few years ago, I was at a party. It was packed with people having a good time. In one of the bedrooms, there were a group of people hanging out.

One of the guys signaled to his girl.

He showed her a small, clear sandwich bag with white powder at the bottom.

His dealer told him it was heroin, but it was roach killer.

They exited the room and walked into a nearby empty bathroom to get high.

He made a joint with the powder, lit it, and shared it with his girl.

After a couple minutes, he asked her, "How are you doing?"

Her eyes closed, and her head tilted back as she exclaimed, "Oh my God. Awesome. I feel amazing."

He agreed, smiled, and took a another hit.

She opened her eyes and looked down at her forearm in the light.

Her expression became alarmed and scared.

Her eyes were convinced they saw large, black spiders with long, black furry legs crawling allover her arm.

She sluggishly reached into a drawer below the sink, grabbed a large nail clipper and extended the long metal cuticle sander with a sharp point.

She looked again at her forearm where again she saw the imaginary spiders everywhere.

It was a scene right out of a horror movie.

She quietly began stabbing her forearm trying to kill those imaginary spiders. With each stab, she punctured a half-inch gash below her skin.

She stabbed her forearm again and again.

Blood squirted upward landing in her hair, splashing on the walls, and hitting her boyfriend.

Her boyfriend was unaware of her actions as much as she was unaware of his. He was just as fucked up.

He moved closer to the mirror to examine his face. His eyes were convinced that a thin, clear plastic film covered his face.

He peered intently into the mirror until he almost touched it.

He scratched his cheek repeatedly to remove the film.

It didn't go away.

He forcefully scratched more and more.

Blood streamed down both his cheeks and forehead.

A friend walked by who saw through an opening in the door what was happening, and took a gasp before he yelled, "Stop! What are you both doing?"

Neither responded.

The friend knocked the nail clippers out of the girl's hand.

Then, he grabbed the guy's hand from his face.

Amid the commotion, others rushed into the room.

Jaws jittered, hands shook, and eyes surveyed the blood splattered everywhere.

Someone shrieked, "Call 911!"

The key point here is drugs can ruin lives.

I have had many girlfriends who complained about my own drug use.

They grieved, "Why are you always high when we are together? Are you looking to escape reality? Is there something wrong with me? Am I not fun enough to hang out? Am I inadequate or lacking in some area?"

I told them, "Me getting high all the time has nothing to do with you. I like to have fun. What is wrong with that? Can I have fun when I am sober? I have no idea."

Eventually, my girlfriends delivered the ultimatum, "Choose me, or choose the Salerno family. You can't have both. They conflict too much."

Then, I always made the same choice, and the girl left.

What I didn't tell them is that I haven't met the right girl yet. A girl so important to me that I would want to change how I live my life for her. I didn't want to hurt their feelings. Am I wrong?

In reality, when I look at all the other guys in the Salerno family, every one of them has a dysfunctional or nonexistent family life. They are all a tragedy.

Another drug to stay away from is nitrous oxide. It comes in 20 pound tanks. Dealers buy bags of balloons from the party supply stores and sell the balloons at summer concert festivals. The ones that last several days.

The nitrous oxide sometimes turns women into sex-crazed maniacs. I once saw a woman try it.

Then, she ripped her clothes off, danced around, and fucked the first guy who said hello to her.

CARLO: How do people do the nitrous oxide inside a balloon?

JOHNNY: You take a deep breath from a balloon and catch an instant 45-60 second buzz off of it.

On the second breath, I've had to take a knee.

On the third breath, my legs and back give out, and I collapse to the ground.

I stare at the sky shifting in different directions like a kaleidoscope. It's great.

CARLO: I thought nitrous oxide makes your voice real high-pitched like a mouse or a chipmunk? It gets you high too?

JOHNNY: You're thinking of helium that makes your voice high. This is different. I'm talking about nitrous oxide.

Have you ever gone to the dentist and had work done when they gave you laughing gas to numb the pain?

Breathing in the gas makes you feel giggly and relaxed. The gas in the dentist office is diluted nitrous oxide. The stuff the dealers put in balloons is 100% pure.

CARLO: How does a dealer get a tank of nitrous oxide?

JOHNNY: The dealer has a caterer's license. They may not have the first clue about how to be a caterer, but the license allows them to buy the nitrous oxide in 20 pound tanks from food distributors.

You know how whipped cream comes in an aerosol can? And how the whipped cream comes out all fluffy at the beginning until the end when it comes out runny?

The nitrous oxide is what makes the whipped cream fluffy. When it runs out of nitrous oxide, the whipped cream gets runny.

Caterers use the tanks to help them make cakes and desserts without having to buy cases and cases of whipped cream cans.

A 20 pound tank can make a few hundred cakes.

The food distributor that sells the tanks to the drug dealer doesn't ask, "Hey, how many cakes are you making with these tanks?"

Dealers can get 100 balloons out of a 20 pound tank that sell for $4 each or $400 in total. The tank gas costs $80 to fill with the gas. It's a nice profit.

They have ambulances at these music festivals on standby for overdoses. People overdose all the time.

The dealers don't feel guilty because they justify it as they can't control it if someone else wants to take too much of what they sell.

Does a beer company feel guilty for someone drinking too much and dying from alcohol poisoning or a drunk driving accident?

The buyer decides how much they drink and what stupid shit they do afterwards.

It's like the gun shop owner who sells a gun to someone who shoots himself. The owner might feel bad for the person who shot himself, but he doesn't feel guilty for selling him the gun.

The gun shop owner didn't intend for anyone to hurt themselves with it. The owner didn't know beforehand that the buyer planned to shoot himself with the gun, right? How could he know?

And even if he suspected something when he was about to sell the gun and then refused to sell it, where do you think the buyer would go next?

He would try to find another gun store across town that would sell to him.

And as for believing dealers cause somebody to overdose. How do you know? Are you a doctor?

How many different drugs does a person do when he or she overdoses?

Nobody just takes one drug.

You can see the point I am trying to make.

At these music festivals, who sells the kids nitrous oxide balloons and every other drug imaginable?

Around here, it is the Outlaws biker gang.

They are able to do this because they run security at the music festivals.

It starts at the front entrance gate. The bikers inspect the bags that kids plan to bring inside with them.

If a kid plans to stay for several days at the festival, it's no surprise the bags have a bunch of personal belongings and probably drugs.

The bikers search the bags with the stated reason that they are looking for drugs. They seize the bags when they find them and throw them in the back of a rented semi-trailer.

At a typical festival, they fill up at least three semi-trailers with confiscated bags. They go through the bags after the festival and sell what they can.

The kids never complain to the police because they think the bikers doing security are the police.

The big benefit of confiscating the bags is the kids lose their drugs, and they enter the festival looking to buy.

The bikers have people inside the festivals that sell drugs.

Last month, my pirates, Schnaze and Lucky Charms, went to one of those music festivals and stole the bikers' semi-trailers.

Schnaze wanted the trucks for his fleet. He could care less about the bags inside.

The bikers got stuck with the bill for the trucks.

They suspected, but weren't sure if Schnaze and Lucky did it.

Hey, did you hear about the hookah shop owned by the same biker gang in Ozone Park that was blown up last week?

The store wasn't paying their tax to the Salerno Family and sold some meth that killed a connected guy's sister.

The Salerno family waited until the bikers stopped by the store.

When they did, two Salerno guys with machine guns were posted on the roof of the store and aimed their guns at the back door.

The Salerno guy who lost his sister parked in front of the store and walked inside holding a Molotov cocktail.

With a tear in his eye, he pulled out a lighter, and paused for a moment as he stared intently at the bikers.

He decried, "This is for you, you fucks!"

He lit the cocktail and threw it at the walls that immediately went up in flames.

The bikers reached under the counter, pulled out a pistol, and shot the guy three times.

He collapsed on the sidewalk outside the store as flames engulfed inside the store.

To escape, the bikers ran out the back door into the alley.

On the roof, the Salerno guys opened fire, mowing the bikers down.

Then, there was an explosion inside the store, and burning debris landed on the dead bikers.

This isn't the first time we had a beef with the Outlaws.

Now there is a war between the Outlaws and the Salerno family. We are a lot bigger than them, so I'm not worried.

BLAST OFF

June 22, 2015

Hey, speaking of drugs, I am in the mood for some DMT. I'll call my guy.

CARLO: What is DMT?

JOHNNY: Dimethyltryptamine is abbreviated as DMT. It is a substance found in all living things.

Our body releases it when we dream and when we die.

When we die, DMT is the drug that blasts us off from Earth to heaven, or, in my case, to more sinister places.

You probably heard the story when some people die for a short time.

Then, they are brought back to life.

These people claim they felt like they left their body and they were going to heaven? That experience is caused by DMT.

DMT is made from the root bark of a plant found in Central and South America. The plant is called Mimosa Hostilis. They dig up the root ball of the plant and remove a purple colored bark, powder it or soak it, and they may add chemicals to it.

When people smoke it, DMT gives them the ability to dream while they are awake.

The trip can last about 15-20 minutes. This is just enough time for people to get high on their lunch breaks at regular jobs.

I think this ability to dream while awake is pretty cool.

I look at dreams as a way to look beyond my own limitations. I believe I control my own limitations.

Trying DMT takes guts because most people are afraid to experience what they don't understand.

Most people don't want to lose control of their mind for a short time.

Did you ever take the time to reflect on the fact that when we sleep our dreams take over our consciousness?

The irony is we don't think we control what happens in our dreams, but we do.

The part that blows my mind the most is not only does our mind create the world we experience in our dreams, but our mind controls both the choices we make, and the outcomes of those choices.

CARLO: What about nightmares?

JOHNNY: DMT can cause nightmares. I've known people who tremble in fear the entire time they trip.

Sometimes they remember, sometimes they don't, just like regular dreams and nightmares.

I haven't seen anyone get addicted to it. People usually do it every once in a while as an alternative to LSD.

DMT is not that popular of a drug due to the nightmare possibility.

My last DMT trip was a tough one.

All of the sudden I heard a loud crash and cops kicked in the front door of my house. The cops were dressed in black robes with hoods like grim reapers. They charged toward me and threw me to the ground.

Usually, I dream that other wiseguys kick in my door.

I realized that in the line of work I have chosen, I can't live happily ever after. No matter how much good I think I do for other people, the cops have a grudge against me.

I hope tonight's dream is better.

I know it is midnight, but when I need it, I got to have it, five grams, enough for 50 hits.

If you weren't so young, I would invite you to join me and get ready to blast off!

You wouldn't be able to say no to my invitation.

I use the term "blast off" because I feel like I am about to launch into outer space. Soon, I will able to turn around and look at the my own world like an astronaut would looking back at planet Earth.

Hey, how is your weed business going?

CARLO: One truth I am learning is that the more product I push on to the people who distribute it, the more they can sell.

The challenge is getting them to accept the additional product. I found that playing distributors and dealers off one another is an effective tactic.

I create competition where none existed previously.

I say things like, "I am going to have to cut you back on shipments because this guy down the street is doing really well. He moves stuff quicker than you and pays a slightly higher price."

The dealer says, "What do you mean cut me back?"

I reply, "Cut you back on the premium stuff, I can replace it with the lower quality stuff."

The dealer pleads with me, "Premium hydro is what everyone wants and next to nobody has your quality around here. Where do you get it? The hydro you have is better than the Mexican or California stuff."

I don't tell him about my supplier in Canada on the St. Lawrence River.

I ask him, "What can I do? My hands are tied."

Then, the dealer begs, "What is the other guy moving?"

I confide in him, "I shouldn't tell you, but you are a good friend of mine."

The dealer promises, "You have my word; I need to know."

I give him a little data, "the guy down the street is moving about +30% more than you a week."

The dealer commits, "I'll move +40% more!"

Also, to further answer your question about how my drug business is doing, it doesn't hurt that the guys who work for me fear the Salerno family.

This means they don't have to fear me personally.

From time to time, I go with my guys on deliveries. I tell them they do a good job, and I can tell they like me.

I tell them, "You know, you guys keep doing good, and all of you will have your own route one day. What do you say about all of us going to Atlantic City this weekend, my treat."

I take them to strip clubs and the girls dancing around my guys have their hands all over them. My guys love it.

They say stuff to me like, "You're the best. Can I have the petite red head?"

I don't participate while my guys are in their private rooms. I sit at the bar, light a cigar, tune out the music and girls, and watch the New

York Knicks game playing. I want them to have a good time.

JOHNNY: Beautiful.

PAWN SHOP GOLD

October 23, 2015

JOHNNY: Have you ever met Tony Scams?

CARLO: No. Who is he?

JOHNNY: I'll tell you a little about him. His name is Tony Marucci, but he goes by his nickname, "Tony Scams."

He is a low-level identity thief, business hacker/antagonist, and scumbag. He is connected to Lucky Charms.

Tony had a gal who was the love of his life. He was always insecure that she dated him because he took her out on expensive dates and gave her lavish gifts. I told him that's partially true, you can't be that good to women or they take advantage of you.

She broke up with him to marry another guy and had a kid, but the guy was a deadbeat. They couldn't pay their bills. They moved out of their house into a small apartment. Times were tough.

Tony talked with her, and gave her $500 in cash to help. He said, "Go buy some groceries for you and your baby."

She was so thankful.

After a few more talks and cash gifts, she wanted to say thank you in a way that Tony would appreciate. She met him at a motel for afternoon sex.

Then, it continued every Tuesday and Friday afternoon for four hours. Tony supported her family being the good guy he is.

Tony boasted, "I'm glad I didn't marry her. The relationship we have right now is everything I ever wanted!"

One more story about Tony and women he chases.

He loves talking to lesbian couples where he tries a combination of pickup lines that work more often than not.

After Tony makes casual conversation for a while, he hits them with, "Can I ask you both a personal question? I'm embarassed to ask it, but I need help with something I am not very good at. And I thought who would we better to ask about this topic than two women."

They ask him, "What is it you want to know?"

He shyly murmurs, "What is the best way to eat a woman out?"

They usually giggle.

Then, he quickly asks, "Would you mind showing me? I promise I will just watch to learn."

They reply, "You are not allowed to touch."

He meekly nods his head in agreement.

But when they all get together, 15 minutes into it, Tony inquires, "Can I make sure I am getting the technique right?"

They usually agree, and Tony ends up banging them both.

The other day I asked Tony, "Do you get to see them again after the first night's lesson?"

He says, "Of course, they call me over all the time!"

I'll tell you a little more about Tony. He graduated from home robbery as a teenager to insurance fraud to computer hacking.

He graduated from home robbery as a teenager to insurance fraud to computer hacking.

Tony used to reminisce about when he was a teenager how he could knock off 70 homes a week.

He regularly boasted, "I ran circles around the old guys. They couldn't keep up with me. They could barely do 20 houses a week before they got out of breath. I'm a legend."

For years, he paid a gay waiter at an expensive restaurant in Manhattan to provide him 20 credit card numbers a week for $50 per number. Tony had a credit card machine that could print the cards.

He used the credit cards to purchase things like gold and silver from pawn shops. Precious metals keep their value.

Last week, we saw a hell of a game sitting in his courtside seats. We must have ordered 10 beers each from the waitress. The players almost fell on us a couple times.

I don't remember the fourth quarter. I started regaining my senses on the car ride home.

Tony tells me how his identity theft business is expanding. Tony is an innovator.

He asked me, "You know those new credit cards with the chips inside them?"

I answer, "Of course. That is all I use now."

Tony continued, "I have this new EMV chip that can be put into a plastic credit card to trick the new chip credit card terminals. I applied it to 400+ numbers and put over $2 million in my pockets.

I travel to the Philadelphia and Boston area pawn shops because my massive gold purchases are raising too many eyebrows around here.

I need to buy more full-size safes to put in my basement bedroom! Hopefully, I don't get robbed and they throw me in one of the safes! Who would find me? When I was found, how bad would I stink?"

He tells me about his diesel fuel business.

He buys large quantities of diesel fuel with the bogus credit cards that he sells to Lucky Charms at a discount who then resells it to other people, including Schnaze, and the Russian Mafia to keep their truck fleets running.

Tony goes on vacation to Vegas with his bogus cards.

He stays in the best rooms, eats at the best restaurants, drinks like a fish, buys the best whores, and gambles like a whale.

At the Vegas McCarran airport on his way back to New York, Tony hits the high end, tax-free, luxury goods stores.

He buys huge bags of cigarette jumbo packs, and high-end alcohol gift boxes. The gift boxes have these great, decorative ornament shot glasses. Also, he buys jumbo-size designer perfume/cologne. Each box can cost up to $450 each.

Then, he sells it all on eBay.

eBay is the place where guys like Tony sell their stolen stuff.

The pawn shops hate eBay. They say, "Hey, you took my business!"

I wonder how many other wiseguys move their stolen stuff on that website.

Part of the reason that decent and honest people shop on eBay is because they think they are getting a deal.

I would like to ask them, "Where do you think these deals are coming from?"

When Tony is at home on a regular day, he hits a Waldbaum's Supermarket for $500 in gift cards at the self-checkout lane. $500 is the max amount giftcard he can buy at the terminal.

The self-checkout terminal is a godsend to guys like Tony. There is no cashier to worry about recognizing that he regularly buys giftcards.

Then, Tony goes to Home Depot and buys another $500 in giftcards.

Tony spends entire days going from one place to another burning out credit cards on gift cards.

Laundering stolen money is a full-time job!

Another stop throughout the day that Tony makes is at the post office.

Tony buys stamps with the stolen cards from the self-service stamp machine instead of going to the counter.

Then, he sells all that shit on eBay as well. Of course, he sells it at a discount.

The Postal Inspector busted him five years ago. The inspector announced to the media, "We finally have captured the criminal we call, The Stamp Man."

They gave him a name like a Super Hero or something.

The feds didn't figure out that Tony is also Perfume Man, Cologne Man, Cigarette Man,

Gift Card Man, Credit Card Man, Gold Man, etc. Can you believe it?

When Tony bought things with his own legitimate credit card, he had scams for that too.

One time, he ordered six slot machines online at $1,200 each.

The UPS guy came with the six machines and rang his doorbell.

Tony didn't answer on purpose.

Tony watched carefully from a crack in an upstairs bedroom window.

The UPS guy left the machines on the driveway.

Then, Tony put the machines in his huge basement.

This was when Tony scammed the website.

He called the customer service number and bolstered, "Where are my slot machines? I never received them! I want a refund!"

The customer service associate did some research and confirmed the machines had been delivered.

She asked him, "Are you sure you didn't receive the machines?"

Tony yells, "No, I don't have them!"

She then apologized and offered to resend him six more machines.

He thought for a moment. Then, he replied, "OK, but don't lose them this time!"

You should see Tony's basement. It is setup like a casino. He invites people over to play the slots and makes a lot of money off it.

Another scam Tony has mastered is insurance fraud.

He has been paid for the same garage door 10 times over. I'm not joking. Here's how it works.

He has a network of low-life's who claim to their insurance company that their car backed into Tony's garage door when they visited his house.

As long as Tony's friends make the claims at different auto insurance companies, the scam always works.

The insurance adjusters go out to Tony's house to inspect the damage and complete the required paperwork.

One week later the checks arrive for $3,000 covering each claim. He splits the money with his scumbag helpers.

Tony used to say, "My biggest challenge is making sure I don't make the appointments with the adjusters too close together where they bump into each other at my house looking at the same garage door!"

Another skill Tony has is he makes the highest quality counterfeit passports. He can hack the State Department!

He tells his customers, "Do you know how hard it is to travel seamlessly throughout the world with a fake identity in a post 9-11 environment?"

Then, Tony shrugs his shoulders and sighs, "It's tough even for me. I'll see what I can do for you. But be prepared, this will cost you a lot more than it did previously."

Tony targets big companies and corporations too.

He hates them and regularly fucks with them.

He defends his actions when he claims, "Years ago, I tried pursuing a regular paying decent job. I had no problem making an honest living, but no company would hire me.

It's their fault. They forced me to steal for a living."

Tony favorite hobby is to hack into company databases and poke around. He will change their direct deposit forms to pay the wrong vendors and put bogus shit into their press releases.

Tony is famous for changing public scripted statements for CEOs of large companies right before an investor conference call with Wall Street.

One time, a CEO meant to say, "we apologize for our big miss." But Tony changed the script to say, "we apologize for our big tits."

Tony played a tape of it all the time at my bar to get a laugh.

Last week, Tony claimed, "I have a new crime for the 21st Century."

He paused and then boasted, "I rob data centers."

I asked, "What is a data center?"

He answered, "It is where companies keep their sensitive data like customer information. They store it on servers. Servers are expensive."

I asked, "How expensive are they?"

He replied, "I hit one data center last month with $800,000 in servers, and I sold them for $50,000 on eBay."

I asked him, "What did you do with the sensitive data on the server?"

He scratched his head, "I left it on there. Fuck them."

I asked him, "What if the people who bought it turn you into the company through eBay?"

He laughed, "I used an alias PayPal account. I'm invisible. I am always invisible!"

Lately, Tony has been poking around the email account of the Russian mobster, Alexei Dobrinov.

I work with Dobrinov on things like keeping the Brooklyn cops off his back and he sells me his Eastern European whores at a discount.

Tony was spooked by what he found.

He said Dobrinov is working with a guy named Zhukov in Russia on hacking American companies and government institutions.

Tony said Zhukov is a complete psychopath.

Carlo, you're smart. I want you to spend some time with Tony and learn about this Zhukov crap and more importantly learn how Tony hacks. He offered to teach you.

I want you to learn a new skill as part of a new direction I want to take the family.

The world is changing out there, faster every day, and we are not. Our family has done the same thing the same way for over a hundred years.

If we want to survive another hundred years, we have to change, find many new ways to make money, and find new partners. Develop new skills.

I want you to learn new skills. This isn't going to happen overnight, but I want you to start working on it.

We look to the past to feel good about ourselves when we should be looking forward to the future.

It is not that anyone has done anything wrong.

Many of us including me have allowed ourselves to become stuck in our ways.

When I look at how we operate, I get frustrated.

A guy calls, and we take the bet.

We sell weed and drugs person to person with cash.

We rely on old income sources that are declining every year like construction, union cards, trash removal, and extortion.

The new direction will be good for us.

Work with Tony and learn as much as you can.

Hopefully, we can use that new income to develop more legitimate income sources.

Tony is being watched by a lot of other organizations.

We are in a treacherous business.

Tony throws his money around.

People notice. People talk.

Tony was abducted last month. It scared the shit out of him.

Tony was with some ladies walking in Times Square when a large black Mercedes van pulled in front of them.

The cargo door flew open, and four men from behind grabbed and pushed Tony so fast into the van that his head snapped back sharply.

Due to Tony's inebriated state, his head smacked against the van floor.

The four men were dressed in black with face masks. One captor made the symbol with one hand for the Italian horns, the Italian symbol for death, by extending his first and fourth fingers straight, bending his second and third fingers, and covering them with his thumb.

With his other hand, the captor pulled out a 20" long by 6" inches wide hunting knife with a wooden handle shaped like a pistol grip.

He shook the Italian horns at Tony slowly as he spoke with a hateful tone, "Take a look at my knife! Now take a look at this jar! Do you know what is inside this jar?"

The captor smashed the jar against Tony's head.

Tony's head was soaked in the jar's formaldehyde.

A severed penis plopped into Tony's lap.

Tony screamed in horror as he realized some guys penis was sitting in his lap.

Then, Tony squealed like a little girl, crying out at the top of his lungs fearing for his life.

He sensed that this is a mob hit.

Tony's captor yelled, "Shut the fuck up or I'm going to cut your prick off right now! Get Godzilla from the back of the van!"

One captor pulled off a blanket covering Godzilla's cage and threatened, "We haven't fed this gator for three days!

First, you are going to lose a hand to the gator.

You can pick which hand!

Then, you are losing your prick!

Balls and all!

You fuck!"

Tony pleads, "Please! Please! No! Anything! Whatever you want!"

The captor calmly orders, "Where is the fucking gold and money?!

I want to go there right now!

Or you lose a hand and your prick!"

THE MOB LAWYER

November 10, 2015

JOHNNY: I have to stay out of trouble since my lawyer has been coming under heat from the feds. The feds opened a case on him and it doesn't look good.

CARLO: What happened?

The U.S. Attorney has finally grown a set of balls to start the process to take down my guy that they call the "mob lawyer."

He represents me, Al, Schnaze and Lucky Charms in addition to every other top mobster or criminal in New York City for the past twenty years.

His record on murder trials is flawless.

He represented the key defendant in the last 23 high profile murder trials, and my lawyer won every single one!

He certainly didn't make any friends in the Justice Department over the years.

I can't count how many U.S. Attorney and Assistant U.S. Attorney careers has he ended by winning all those cases?

Even if my guy loses a case, he only loses it temporarily. He always ends up winning.

Look what happened with me on my last case.

The FBI handed the U.S. Attorney enough evidence to put me away for the rest of my life.

I got convicted, went away to jail, and my lawyer works his magic.

He gets the government's star witness to recant his testimony from my trial.

On my appeal, I received immediate release, and their star witness went to jail for perjury!

The FBI agents probably grumbled, "That son of a bitch lawyer has shot holes in most every investigation we brought forward to the Justice Department! Enough is enough. We're investigating him!"

It's understandable for the agents to be pissed off that my lawyer represents real criminals who they see as belonging in jail for the next 20, 30 or 40 years.

Instead, my lawyer gets his clients off with tiny or no sentences.

Also, the agents can't help but notice that before, during or after every major case my guy defends, one or all of the Justice Department lawyers on the case magically accept a position earning big bucks with a private sector, top tier law firms in Manhattan.

No one asks why this happens?

Other than the obvious reason that it is really hard for a government lawyer to support a family on the modest income, you can see where I am going with this.

My guy is a master of the good old boy network.

Every big shot lawyer in Manhattan is his friend.

He picks up the phone, calls one of his pals with whom he plays golf, drinks, attends charity or sporting events, or knows from this or that place, and asks him for a favor.

The call goes something like this, "Hey buddy, can you hire a piece of shit Justice Department attorney who is a major thorn in my client's side?"

He continues, "If you can do this favor for me, I will owe you my friend. I'll give you a cut of the half million from my retainer on the case."

Then, the big shot lawyer doing the favor asks, "Where should I put the guy when I hire him?"

To which my guy replies, "Who cares? Have him work on pro bono or divorce cases for the next six to twelve months before you get rid of him."

The FBI agents want to put an end to those conversations and did an investigation on my lawyer.

The investigation originally was about a Midtown condo building project where my lawyer had made a personal investment.

The developer of the building rehabbed the condos and sold most of the condos to fraudulent buyers.

It was a weak link trying to tie my lawyer to the mortgage fraud case. They had no evidence that he or the developer knew fraudulent buyers bought the condos.

At the time, if the FBI had brought their investigation forward to a grand jury, the jury would have said, "Why are you wasting our time with this?"

Fast forward to a few months ago, when the same developer was indicted on a separate IRS tax fraud case that had nothing to do with the condo building project.

On this case, the developer was looking at 20 years.

The U.S. Attorney from the mortgage fraud investigation offered to help him on his tax fraud case, only if he cooperated against my lawyer.

It's no surprise the developer buckled under the pressure, and claimed my lawyer knew the loans to the condo buyers were fraudulent.

The investigation became a real case and headed to a grand jury.

The people who received the fraudulent loans were listed on the indictment.

The two FBI agents visited him to drop-off a "target letter" stating he was being named a "person of interest" on the fraudulent loans case.

A felony conviction on his record meant my lawyer would be disbarred.

My lawyer told the agents, "This is bullshit. The U.S. Attorney has no case. I can beat this in any court with any judge. Here is my lawyer's information. Please ask the U.S. Attorney to contact him in regards to this case."

I find it entertaining and hilarious that the most powerful and connected lawyer in New York City has a lawyer.

From my lawyer's point of view, he figured he spent his entire career getting real criminals off on cases that were ten times more rock solid with evidence than the mortgage fraud case.

Mortgage fraud was peanuts compared to winning murder cases. How could he lose?

My lawyer had a tough day in court today with the mortgage fraud trial.

It has to feel odd for him to be in the seat of the defendant.

The U.S. Attorney had my lawyer sitting right next to the mortgage fraud guys during the trial.

Even though my lawyer never met the mortgage fraud guys ever in his life before this trial, the US Attorney insisted on them sitting together.

By doing that, it looks to the jury like everyone is guilty by association.

I asked Schnaze to be there all day today to let me know how things went.

The last two weeks focused on all the evidence being presented against the guys who did the fraudulent mortgage loans. This evidence has nothing to do with my lawyer. Today, the U.S. Attorney switched gears and put the spotlight on my lawyer.

There were three bad bomb shells today for my lawyer.

First, the US Attorney flashed up on the screen my lawyer's 1040 tax form from last year.

My lawyer goes nuts, telling his lawyer, "That son of a bitch can't do this. Object! Object!"

Both sides begin making arguments to the judge for and against the 1040 being up on the screen.

My lawyer's 1040 had income of $4.8 million listed on it. Every second the 1040 was up on the screen, it might have helped the jury believe, "hey, this guy got rich off the condo building fraudulent loans!"

How much of the $4.8 million your lawyer made last year was from the condo building?

It was small in comparison to his total income, something like $300,000. My lawyer made a lot more off working on Al's case.

The $300,000 amount never came out in court.

After the judge ordered the 1040 taken down, the US Attorney threw up the second bombshell on the screen.

The screen was illuminated with pictures of wiseguys. My photo was enlarged at the top of the screen.

Then, the U.S. Attorney yelled, "Ladies and gentlemen of the jury, the number one lawyer to the criminal underworld of New York City sits at the table among the defendants! Many of his current and former clients are convicted felons from the Salerno Crime Family including the crime family boss, Johnny Toracio!"

He objected; however, the damage was done. The judge advised the jury to strike that statement from consideration.

The final bombshell of the day, the third one, was the biggest one of all.

The U.S. Attorney called the developer who did the condo building project up to sit in the witness stand.

My lawyer barely knew him. If anyone was aware of the fraudulent mortgages, it would have been the developer, not my lawyer.

The US Attorney asked the developer, "Can you please identify for the courtroom the mastermind behind the fraudulent loans perpetrated by the defendants?"

The developer shook his finger violently, pointed directly at my lawyer, leaned forward in his chair, and yelled at the top of his lungs, "He is the criminal mastermind! He manipulated all of us to do this unspeakable crime! Right there he sits! He is responsible for everything!"

The whole courtroom went silent. Several women put an open hand against their mouth as they appeared to gasp for a breath.

My lawyer panicked and could be heard by those seated around him blurting out to his lawyer, "Fix this, you son of a bitch!"

It wasn't difficult to figure out what conclusions the jury drew from today's bombshells. My lawyer is done. Stick a fork in him. He's fried, burnt.

He had it coming though.

He became a marked man with the Justice Department when he got so many of us wiseguys and criminals off for so many years with probation or light sentences.

Many times, he was able to get the charges dismissed - even when we were guilty of crimes, and we expected and should have gone to jail.

Quite frankly, at the time, we didn't care how he did it, but we were thankful to him for it.

The man who made a mockery of the criminal justice system over his legal career was served up the same level of mockery on his day of reckoning.

Hey, let's change subjects, how is your gambling business going?

CARLO: The best leads come from my favorite golf course. I transitioned from being a caddy to being a decent golfer. The guy who works the front desk and does the golf reservation tee times gives me tips when a couple guys need an extra golfer to fill a tee time.

I receive a text or call from him, "I got a 9:30 tomorrow morning with two lawyers, you want to join them?"

Then, the next day, I start out with a serious game for a few holes. Next, I'm talking about sports with them.

I say, "You see the game last night? Can you believe so and so did so and so?"

That gets them going. Pretty soon, they are placing bets with me.

Legitimate guys, doctors, lawyers, bankers, Wall Street gurus, and professionals are my client list. Others in the family are always asking for my list so they could take over my operation or, worst case, shake them down. I put them off.

A business executive I golf with asked for a lawyer recommendation for a big problem he is having.

I recommended your lawyer to him.

He took $24 million in personal loans from his company. All $24 million was cash in his pockets.

He paid no taxes on the money because it was a loan. He thought what he did was legal.

The funny thing is taking the loans is legal as long as he paid the money back via monthly payments.

But he didn't make any payments.

The IRS did a routine audit and saw the personal loans on his company's books.

They asked questions.

He stated adamantly that he never tried to hide the loans.

The IRS left for several months. He thought he was OK, but they returned and threatened charging him with tax fraud.

JOHNNY: I don't believe what he told you about thinking the personal loans were legitimate.

He knew what he was doing. He is a criminal, just like us. He can't bullshit me.

Even if he pays the money back, he is still going to jail for a while.

Even though he may offer to pay the taxes and penalties, what he did is still a crime.

The old saying applies, "You do the crime, you do the time."

It's like if you rob a bank, and pay the money back. You still go to jail, right?

The thing that chaps my ass about your friend is here is some rich guy who owns a company and probably is making a very decent living, and he decides he wants to make even more, tax-free.

Isn't that a textbook definition for greed?
We're all guilty of it though.

THE SCORE

I followed up on Johnny's request for me to meet with Tony Scams to find out more about the Russians and learn hacking.

Before we went to his house, Tony wanted to take me to Lincoln Center. He loved operas.

The entire time he sat in his chair enthralled, seized and captivated by the music.

He said to me afterwards, "The music sounds like it is sailing through the wind and crashing into the walls of the music hall."

Then, he added, "Most importantly, the music signifies and embodies power in life. Power over other living beings. The kind of power I exert to gain greater influence in the future."

Tony had a big house on the water in the exclusive suburb of Bayport on Long Island.

November 15, 2015

TONY: Carlo, remember that "He that waits upon fortune is never sure of dinner."

Benjamin Franklin said that, one of the founding fathers of this great country.

You want to hear a funny story?

Take a look at the two paintings in my living room facing each other on opposite walls.

You see the painting with the four terrorists?

They have tears running down their faces.

Their terrorist dear friend is lying dead on the ground with a large red hole shot in his chest and his body surrounded by blood.

This is very sad, right?

Take a look at the opposite wall. Here we have another painting of a beautiful mountainside with large mature trees and a picturesque creek that runs through a green, grassy meadow populated with groups of thick bushes.

Do you know what the title of this painting is?

The title is, "I'm in here, you fucks!"

There is an American sniper in those fucking bushes! Ha-ha!

Today, we are going to plan a truck heist of merchandise from Dobrinov International. The trucking company owned by the Russians.

CARLO: Johnny didn't mention a truck heist.

TONY: He's on board, don't worry. This will be good training for you.

These Russians need a good lesson taught to them by Tony Scams. They had bad intentions and it is my patriotic duty to put them out of business.

This Friday through Monday, there are over 600 Dobrinov trucks with at least $15 million in merchandise scheduled to be delivered in the Tri-state area.

I looked at what merchandise each truck is scheduled to carry. Some have the latest and greatest televisions and gaming systems. We want those.

They represent 20% of the trucks and 80% of the merchandise value.

If I do the math correctly, the job is worth $12 million in merchandise.

I'll show you how I rerouted the delivery destinations on all 150 trucks to Salerno warehouses in Brooklyn.

I setup enough people to receive the merchandise in the trailers.

Also, I accessed the insurance policy Dobrinov has on his trucks. The policy states that the maximum coverage for merchandise on his trucks lost to events such as hurricane, winter storm, fire, a house or roof collapsing, truck accident, fire, or truck theft is only $5 million.

Twelve million minus five million insurance payout means Dobrinov will be seven million dollars in the hole.

Our heist will put his trucking company into bankruptcy.

Johnny will be able to buy Dobrinov's company for pennies on the dollar.

I have a list of all Dobrinov's trucking customers and what Dobrinov charges them.

We will solicit Dobrinov's customers after the heist.

We will undercut what Dobrinov charges them.

We'll have Schnaze use his trucking company to handle the accounts until we can get our hands on all of Dobrinov's trucks.

CARLO: This will be a large legitimate business for the Salerno family.

TONY: Whenever I hack, it feels like electricity runs through my veins.

CARLO: How do you hack into companies?

TONY: I am amazed at the amount of information available on the internet that is just waiting to be stolen.

The only security for a company in this day and age is a false sense of security. No one is safe.

The culprit is the open architecture of the internet. Most companies have hundreds of routers, switches, firewalls and servers that are plugged into the internet.

I learned there are two types of organizations: those that have been hacked, and those that don't yet realize they've been hacked. It takes an average organization over three months to detect they've been hacked. Once they realize it, most organizations don't know what to do about it. Remarkably, most organizations can't even tell what information was stolen.

It is a challenge for companies to safeguard every piece of hardware from being hacked, and most companies fail miserably. If I can't get in through the front door, I use the back door or a window. There are so many choices.

Once I'm in a network, I have encryption software to decrypt any important files I come across.

The encrypted files usually contain sensitive data like personal health records, banking information, 401k retirement plans with account access information, company press releases, new product details and plans, future strategy, etc.

Yesterday, one of the files Dobrinov had in his personal folder didn't even belong to him. It was stolen by his friend Zhukov from a large bank.

The file contained debit card numbers, pin numbers, stock portfolios, and addresses of its wealthiest account holders.

CARLO: How large are the accounts?

TONY: The top ten accounts have over $250,000 in each. There are over 20,000 accounts on the file.

CARLO: What are their plans with the file?

TONY: Steal the money.

CARLO: What was on the second file?

TONY: The second file had paperwork behind an unannounced large merger of two companies.

I believe the Russians will use this information for inside stock trading before the merger is announced and make a boatload of money.

CARLO: What was on the third file?

TONY: The third file has a financial press release for a large auto company. There is a draft of an upcoming press release for its latest quarterly results.

I expect the Russians will use this information to place bets for or against the stock based on whether the information exceeds or falls short of Wall Street analyst expectations.

THE MASK

I could never figure out why such a respectable guy like Thomas Flanagan used to hang out with Johnny and others from the Salerno Family. It didn't make any sense.

Flanagan was from a prominent family. His mother was a Billingsley. Her family owned the largest and most prestigious art auction houses in the world.

His father was from a local New York City auction house family.

He wasn't from Queens. He grew up in a large mansion in Greenwich, Connecticut.

This was the day I would be enlightened as to who Thomas Flanagan really was during a conversation at Johnny's bar.

December 3, 2015

FLANAGAN: My mom's auction house in Midtown is where multi-million dollar art pieces are sold to high net worth individuals and their representatives seated in the audience.

I look for people that stand out as a bidders in the crowd.

One kid I saw the other day had attended a lot of recent auctions.

He was not like the others in the room. They were old. He was young.

They were clean cut and dressed nicely. He sported a beard and khaki shorts.

He looked like a typical Upper East Side spoiled kid spending his parents money buying fine art as a hobby.

Recently, he spent over $10 million in art.

I researched his address. It was a nice townhouse overlooking Central Park.

If you are in the business of stealing art, there is no better place to identify your next score than at an art auction.

I found out the place was empty during the day.

An uncle of mine works for the Secret Service. I borrowed his badge without him knowing and wrote up a fake search warrant.

I went to the building where the townhouse was. I showed my badge and search warrant to the doorman.

I firmly said in an official-sounding voice, "United States Secret Service. We have a search and seize warrant for #IB."

He obligingly responded, "Yes Sir. I believe the owner is not home at this time. Is everything OK?"

I reassured him and let him know this was part of a three-year investigation that I am not privy to share the details of at this time.

Then, the doorman asked, "I have the key. Would you like me to let you in?"

This was music to my ears. I thanked him for his cooperation, gave him a fake business card, and told him I would be in contact over the next several days to gather more information.

As he unlocked the door, he noted, "There is a private alarm system that I do not have the code. It goes directly to the NYPD. I believe this won't be a problem, correct?"

I answered, "Correct, I have notified the NYPD."

He believed me.

I had to work quick. I loaded the best art pieces into my cargo van parked outside.

A NYPD patrol car responded to the security alarm.

I was about to get into my van when the cop car approached and parked behind it.

I hesitated.

The cop in the passenger seat exited the car with his gun drawn, and yelled, "Freeze!"

What did I do?

I walked calmly over to the NYPD car, with both arms extended. In one hand, I showed my Secret Service badge, and in the other, I held out the search warrant.

The cops paused with a stunned look.

I yelled, "United States Secret Service, you are blowing our operation!"

They looked at each other unsure of themselves.

I ordered, "Get back in your car!"

One of the cops reached calmly into his car to shut off the lights.

Then, they drove away.

I'll bet one of the cops said to the other cop, "Another case of the left hand not knowing what the right hand is doing."

Then, at some point later, the cops most likely realized their error and exclaimed, "That son of a bitch tricked us!"

End of conversation dated December 3, 2015

I thought Flanagan was an art dealer. That was bullshit.

He was an art thief who passed himself off to anyone who would believe him as related to a prominent New England art family.

His story was good. Why wouldn't most people believe it? What kind of a person lies about who their mother and father is? Thomas A. Flanagan or whatever his real name is.

I guess I was a little hurt that he felt compelled to lie not only to those in the art world who would believe his story, but even to a gullible teen like me.

Did he do tell his lies for shits and giggles?

When his lies were accepted by the listener did he get a shot of satisfaction or elation?

The weird thing was he kept claiming his parents were in the art business after he revealed his art theft.

I reasoned that he was like an actor who remained constantly in character. He didn't know what was reality and what was not.

However, the art theft story didn't end there.

The next day after Flanagan told it, I received a call from my friend Oso.

He returned from a trip with his Mexican Cartel friends four-wheeling in an ATV across the South Arizona desert.

While the engines roared and the spinning wheels kicked sand high into the air, he had missed a text alert on his phone that was buried deep inside his pocket.

The text alert was titled, "NY Townhouse Alarm."

He told me his doorman had told him how bad he felt about a man he had let inside the townhouse who identified himself as a Secret Service Agent.

Oso was a different kind of robbery victim for Flanagan.

Oso vowed he wouldn't be going to the police for help in finding the thief.

It would have surprised anyone at the art auction house, the most of which being Flanagan, that the kid in khakis and a beard bidding on high-priced art was not a spoiled Upper East Side kid buying art with his parents money as a hobby.

This kid was one of the biggest drug suppliers in New York City.

Oso supplied Maurice.

Maurice was the top drug dealer in Queens and Brooklyn.

Oso kept a low profile, and even in the drug world, outside of Maurice, most never heard of him.

Oso was the man behind the man.

THE RAT

Flanagan ripped off an old lady 25 years his senior he was trying to seduce that he met at an art auction by convincing her to buy art from him.

He gouged her for $860,000 on a painting that cost him $500,000.

She wired the money to his account and he said the painting would be delivered the next day.

Then, he decided to keep the painting and the money. This wasn't the first time he scammed an old lady.

He told her the delivery was delayed.

She called the FBI.

The FBI visited Flanagan's townhouse.

Flanagan was well-known to the FBI. They arrested him on four separate cases for which he did time in jail each time over the course of his 30-year career.

The FBI knocked on his door, "Flanagan, we know you're in there! Let us in."

Flanagan asked, "What do you want?"

The agent answered, "We're here for the painting Flanagan. Don't make a fuss. We know it's you."

Flanagan asked another question, "Agent Bridgeton? Is that you? Sure, my apologies."

Before he opened the door, Flanagan threw the painting out his sliding glass back door into the courtyard he shared with other tenants.

Agent Bridgeton asked, "Flanagan, where is the painting?"

Flanagan replied, "What painting? I have no painting."

There was an awkward silence.

Flanagan's phone rang.

It was the doorman who asked, "Mr. Flanagan, are you looking for a painting? I have it right here. One of the other tenants said it fell off your terrace."

Flanagan held up his hands, and Agent Bridgeton cuffed him.

Agent Bridgeton reassured him, "You know what we are going to ask you, don't you? You always give us the information we need."

Agent Matera continued, "That is how Flanagan avoids long jail sentences. He is our best partner.

We'll put in a good word with the Assistant U.S. Attorney on your case.

This will be your fifth federal case, so you need all the help you can get."

Flanagan muffled, "I can tell you about a big-time drug supplier named Oso and his friends Maurice, Schnaze and Lucky."

Agent Bridgeton added, "We know all about them. Those four are like shooting fish in a barrel. I'm not worried about them.

We need more help on a really big fish. If you can give us Johnny Toracio, then you might just get probation."

RIDING DIRTY

Schnaze and Lucky Charms headed to an apartment in Brooklyn where Maurice had scheduled a meeting.

December 16, 2015

SCHNAZE: Break it down for me how you got us hooked up with Maurice on this buy.

LUCKY: Maurice had harsh words initially when he said, "I had my reservations working with you two meth-mouth fools. You look sloppy. You don't stay on point. Small mistakes turn into big mistakes over time. You dig?"

He continued, "As we work together, I am going to get you all the supplies you need to make your meth. You need anything else like pills, cocaine, weed, heroin, anything, I'm your man."

I told him we were straight, and we would come to him for everything.

I asked for three kilos of cocaine today.

He said, "I got you. I'll give it to you on credit."

We began talking, and Maurice let me know he sells boxes of Sudafed to meth cooks throughout the city.

Sudafed is the key ingredient I need for a bunch of chemical reactions that yield meth. Each box of Sudafed comes with 20 pills, and I can get almost three grams of meth from a box after the chemical reactions.

We can sell the three grams for at least $300.

The cost of each Sudafed box from the drug store or supermarket is about $10. The problem is a person can only buy one box per month, and the places where you can buy it from ask for your driver's license in order to type your information into a database that the DEA reviews regularly for people who buy more than a few boxes a year.

You might think, can't we just go to different drug stores and buy what we need? The answer is no. All the stores share the same database with the DEA. When you buy too many boxes, alarm bells go off, and you're hit.

The DEA is knocking on your door asking you questions.

Getting a large number of boxes means you have to have a large number of people buying them. Maurice has a huge network.

Maurice was charging $50 per box to each meth cook in the city. However, there are only a finite number of boxes Maurice and his people can get their hands on every month. Maurice then splits up what he has among the meth cooks.

He sells 400 boxes per month. Today, we are picking up 200 boxes.

SCHNAZE: How did you get Maurice to give us half of his monthly total on the first buy we are doing with him?

LUCKY: I did something the other meth cooks were not willing to do. I agreed to share more of our profits with him.

Voluntarily, I increased the price per box we pay him from $50 to $100.

Maurice agreed to front us the first 200 boxes and pay him $20,000 after we sell the meth.

He thanked me for helping him out with so much business.

SCHNAZE: When someone pats you on the back, they are probably looking for a soft spot to place the knife!

LUCKY: Agreed. Think big picture for a moment as to why I setup the buy like this.

Maurice controls most of the Sudafed boxes sold in the New York City area. If we can convince him to sell all or most of his boxes to us, what will happen?

SCHNAZE: The other meth cooks will not be able to make meth.

LUCKY: And the street dealers who buy the meth from the cooks will be asking, where's my meth? Go get me meth.

Who will the cooks inquire with about buying meth? Maurice.

We supply Maurice. We corner the market.

We set the price. We can raise the price whenever we want.

Next, I asked Maurice, "What is the highest number of boxes you can get per month? Can you go above 400?"

He thought for a moment and claimed he can get us 1,000 per month.

With that amount, we can sell $300,000 per month. We pay Maurice $100,000, we keep the other $200,000.

The key problem with meth is when we make it, there is the small risk of explosions. I did some research.

There are a lot of different ways to make meth.

I found the safest way, guaranteed. I tried it on some small batches and it worked.

We can use my place until we are up and running. I'll get us a cook house afterwards. Once we corner the market, we can expand to other areas and other drugs.

When we get to the building, Maurice said we are to follow one of his guys standing in the entranceway to underground parking where we will be guided to a parking spot. Then, we'll be escorted up to a 17th floor apartment where Maurice will be waiting.

While we talk to Maurice, his guys will load our car with the merchandise in the garage.

Remember, we'll be riding real dirty when we leave.

If we get caught with this shit, we're facing 15+ years locked up.

SCHNAZE: I'm trusting you with the wheel my brother.

LUCKY: I'm excited about what Maurice can do for us. We live life like a chess game where every move we make we get paid.

LUCKY: We sure do. Hey, how is your new diesel fuel business going?

SCHNAZE: Good. The Russian mobster named Dobrinov owns a huge trucking company. It's a legitimate business.

Tony Scams sells me the diesel at a 50% discount to diesel prices at the fuel stations that I sell to Dobrinov at a 30% discount.

I do three deliveries a week to fill up over 200 trucks Dobrinov has.

BOGUS AS HELL

After Schnaze and Lucky left Maurice's condo, there were 10 cops a quarter mile behind them and another 15 on standby.

December 16, 2015

LUCKY: The cop behind us just flipped on his cherries! Maurice fed us to the sharks! Some partner he is! The feds were waiting to pop us!

SCHNAZE: Drive mother fucker! Bury that needle. Hit the floorboard hard!

LUCKY: I am not spending the next 15 years in jail!

SCHNAZE: Keep your eyes on the road!

You're going to kill us! You don't need to see where the cops are!

Each time you check the rearview mirror, our car swerves. I'm ripping this rearview mirror off and throwing it out of the car!

I'll be the one that checks behind us.

Oh boy, it's not good! There is a trail of cherries!

LUCKY: This car tops out at 140, we're getting close to max speed. No fear!

SCHNAZE: You're going too fast. Watch out, we're coming up on an intersection.

LUCKY: The cops ahead have spikes across the road and sidewalks!

In front of the spikes, two police cars are parked nose to nose blocking both sides of the street!

Oh my God!

SCHNAZE: Are you fucking nuts?

LUCKY: I'm heading for the sidewalk and over the spikes.

(Background noise is multiple thumps and a loud boom).

LUCKY: We hit the spikes. I think only the front right tire popped.

SCHNAZE: There is smoke, sparks and fire coming inside the car from the popped tire. I can't see. Slow down!

None of the cops followed us over the spikes.

The cops are scrambling to move the two police cars parked nose to nose to create an opening for the others to pass through. You could have killed us.

LUCKY: We're losing them.

SCHNAZE: There is too much smoke in here.

LUCKY: Open a window!

SCHNAZE: Pull over! We need to dump this car somewhere and escape on foot.

LUCKY: I'll slow down. We made it brother.

SCHNAZE: You are crazy! You have something wrong in your head. Look at my hands. They won't stop shaking. My nerves are shot. I am freaked out.

LUCKY: One of my partners is just up the road. We can stop there. My partner is bogus as hell like us. He is a coke dealer. When we arrive, don't say anything. I'm calling him now.

(Lucky talks to his phone on speaker).

LUCKY: Hey, it's me. I need a place to hide out for a couple hours. We won't cause you any trouble.

PHONE: I have been listening to the police scanner, mother fucker! Get the fuck away from my house. You are in some serious shit.

LUCKY: We're here. We're parking in back.

PHONE: Bullshit! I am known in this neighborhood. This is the first place the cops will come.

If you knock on my door, I will aim my pistol at your head, cock it, and I am not afraid to fire it! You keep on driving!

(Lucky hangs up phone).

LUCKY: Fucking asshole! I won't forget this!

SCHNAZE: The cops will send everyone they can over to comb through the area.

LUCKY: They can't shut down Brooklyn. They won't find us.

SCHNAZE: I am not sure about that.

LUCKY: I am letting myself get too emotional. There's a subway station. I'm parking.

SCHNAZE: Where will we go? We can't go home.

LUCKY: We'll take the subway to Manhattan, then to Secaucus, then wherever to hide out for a few days.

Then, when things settle down, we are going back to Brooklyn to execute Maurice and his entire crew.

SCHNAZE: You are insane. We don't know if Maurice set us up. The Feds could have been watching us.

LUCKY: Look, Nobody was watching us. Maurice set us up. It was a controlled buy. He is partnered with the Feds.

SCHNAZE: I don't know. Our faces will be all over the news tonight! Where can we go?

LUCKY: We can sleep in the woods, somewhere in North Jersey.

SCHNAZE: Let's put our heads together and think of something.

THE RUSSIAN BLUEPRINT

By this time, Alexei Dobrinov was head of the Russian Mafia in the Brighton Beach neighborhood of Brooklyn. Besides extortion, loan sharking, gambling, and theft, his organization ran a lucrative prostitution and strip club business with Russian and Eastern European women. Most of whom he was able to acquire fake visas and passports to facilitate their extended stays in the United States.

Dobrinov spoke with a heavy Russian accent in a low, deep voice. His black hair slicked back with a three-day beard. He dressed in double-breasted suits with an open collar, colored shirt and he smokes cigars endlessly.

He had a small office in the back of a liquor store with a wooden desk and a color painting of the tyrant dictator Josef Stalin above it.

One of the legitimate businesses he owned was a trucking company.

In the warehouse where Dobrinov kept his trucks, he had a pet Anaconda snake in a cage where everyone could see it. He would exclaim, "I put it right next to the breakroom door where the truck drivers go in and out all day for a coffee. If they screw up a delivery, I'll feed them to the snake! My snake eats rats. You tell on me. You rat on me. You'll end up in the cage!"

I had a few conversations with Dobrinov. He was famous for his disrespect of women.

He would say, "If I get married, it would have to be with a stupid and simple woman, because a great man like myself must dedicate himself to his work. I can't be encumbered by a woman who questions me."

If Dobrinov met someone he didn't like, he would threaten, "In my country, I would throw you in a pot and make soup out of you!"

His partner Zhukov was an entirely different story.

He was located outside of Moscow in a secluded, heavily wooded area in a large warehouse with a single road leading to it.

At the entrance to the road was a metal power gate with five security personnel standing guard holding semi-automatic rifles in a small stone building.

Along the road leading up to the warehouse were tall poles flying flags that had a black skeleton key in the center surrounded by a gold circle and dark blue background.

At first glance, most would consider this a top secret military or government installation, but this place was far from it. It was the headquarters of Zhukov and his organization.

Inside the warehouse, over 1,000 people busily worked at desks on computers and shared information in small groups. The warehouse floor plan was the size of two football fields.

Up above the people working along one wall of the warehouse was a second floor where Zhukov's office was located and a cat walk where he could view his people below him.

On the opposite wall from Zhukov's office that everyone in the building can see is a massive 100-foot-wide by 50-foot-high map of the world with Zhukov's flag above it.

Zhukov spoke with Dobrinov on the phone.

December 17, 2015

ZHUKOV: What we are creating will last forever! Our palaces that are waiting to be built – your palace, and my palace – will be handed down to our successors for generations to come!

Today, we examine the evidence of what remains of the Roman empire from 2,000 years ago, what we find is their magnificent stone structures endured! After we seize power, I want to build the largest and most magnificent stone structures that the world has ever seen.

We will not build any structures out of glass and steel like what other buildings are constructed of today. Those materials disintegrate over time!

Make no mistake, I don't expect our movement to decline like the Romans did after a few hundred years. No. That is not our destiny!

Glory awaits us! I wish you could look at all of our people here supporting our movement. Two years ago, it was you and I. Next year, we will number in the millions. Five years from now, we will have billions of people!

What we are building will be so much more than what we have today.

Today, we have accomplished our initial goal of becoming the worldwide leader in computer hacking.

Next, we will develop the capabilities to disrupt the status quo across all nations and all continents.

The status quo has to be disrupted. The world is too dysfunctional. There is too much bloodshed. There are too many competing ideologies and religions. There is too much industrialization and pollution. There are too many weapons of war.

Our vision is bold. We will build a single world government that unites all people everywhere, all of humanity, under one leader, one flag, one religion, and one movement. Our movement.

We reject all other ideologies and religions. We've developed our own that we are ready to share with the world. How glorious and noble are our efforts!

We are getting close to being able to disrupt the current governments of the world. We will remove their ability to maintain safety and security for their citizens!

We will engineer the collapse of their currencies, banking systems, power grids, satellites, communications, military, and transportation systems. We will engineer chaos!

We will attack the largest governments first: the United States, China and Russia. Once we have control of these, then we will exert our power and influence over the remaining smaller countries. We will seize as much wealth as possible while we do it!

From this chaos, we will emerge as the one solution that can reestablish safety and security for the world. We will also control most of the world's wealth when we are complete.

This building will be the future central bank for all of humanity. From here, we will launch a new digital world currency and financial system.

Then, we will launch the new world government. We will rid ourselves of all weapons of war by disposing of them.

The nuclear ones will be destroyed first. We will stop the unsustainable industrialization that is destroying our planet.

We will save humanity from itself!

We are getting ahead of ourselves. Let's step back for a moment. We are currently slowly and methodically building a database of files and information that prove to be helpful to advance our progress and seize wealth.

However, we overlooked advancing our expertise in being able to unlock or decrypt many of the important files we acquire.

It does us no good to have every secret in the world if we can't unlock the files to read and exploit them to further our movement!

Just as we engineered and innovated our hacking excellence in short order, we will do the same with our decryption capabilities. We will forge this new key with the help of others!

Once we do, we will be able to move trillions of dollars, yuan, rubles and Euros to our accounts and control.

We must move faster! We are too slow!

We are on the right side of history.

We will manage the world's wealth better than anyone else could.

I have work to do in the United States.

I will come visit you, my dear friend Dobrinov!

MIDNIGHT GOODBYE

I received the call to meet Johnny at the Four Seasons Hotel where he had the Penthouse suite with six hookers. Johnny had pleaded out a racketeering charge.

December 24, 2015

JOHNNY: I am saying my final goodbyes to everyone. I fully expected to serve my time as a man, with honor and nobility. I made no deals with the government. I was never a rat. I am a standup guy and live by the code of silence, Omerta.

I remember the feds telling me during my case, "look, we will cut your sentence in half, if you will just admit there is a LaCosa Nostra."

At my sentencing hearing, the prosecutor stated verbally in court that I was the boss of the Salerno family, but in the paperwork for my case, I was referred to as the "boss of an organization."

There was no mention of the Salerno family or La Cosa Nostra. I wouldn't allow any mention of it, and I was ready to accept the consequences of this decision like a man.

CARLO: Boss, they don't make wise guys like you anymore.

JOHNNY: Oh yes, they do. I'm looking at one of the finest examples.

Tomorrow, I go to jail and I may never see you again.

You have no idea how many close friends I've lost over the years. How many relationships with good women I've screwed up? How many hookers I've screwed. How many lives I've helped, and how many lives I've ruined.

CARLO: You've helped more than you've hurt. People respect you, I respect you.

JOHNNY: In Florida, the palm trees stay green year-round. I wish I could see them again.

When I'm 90 years old and I look back at my life, I hope to say I made a lot of bad choices, but I got better at my choices as I grew older.

Why didn't I choose to spend my days on a beach, smoking a cigar, and drinking a martini with a special woman next to me. A woman I could be devoted to?

A 20-year sentence at my age is a long time.

Listen, I'll do what I can for you when I'm away, but you are on your own now.

The kids running things like my son Al are too flashy, and they will end up in jail soon as well.

When I saw you on the street late on Christmas night, I knew you were special. Something caused me to invite you into my bar.

You weren't the first homeless kid who lived in the neighborhood that I had seen, but I picked you for some reason. Call it divine intervention.

Every lesson I taught you over the last few years was to prepare you for this moment.

You are the biological son I could only hope for.

I knew your father. I see a lot of him in you, but you take more after your mother. She was really smart and careful, before the drugs took a hold of her.

You have always made me proud, and I know your parents are looking down at this very moment so very proud of who you became despite all the tragedies and setbacks that beset you early in life.

I wish I could have brought you into a more honest life, but this life is all I know.

Make sure your kids grow up to live legitimate lives.

I am aware that I live an insane life. Al's mother was my first love. At the time, I was just getting started. I was only 18. I was too young, dumb and immature. I was not ready for a family. I didn't know any better.

I skipped town for a while after he was born. This was one of the biggest mistakes I made in my life.

We all have our crosses to bear. It's important to keep what's important first. I didn't do that. I apologize for dumping this all on you today and here.

My life is reaching its sunset. I choose not to change it at this point.

Power corrupts people if you let it.

I remember when you were fourteen years old, you had a good reputation for doing little jobs for people.

I asked you to go to the deli to get big sandwiches for the rest of the bosses. It was the middle of the afternoon and all of them were in the bar.

One boss said, "Pastrami, thinly sliced. Last time, another kid brought the sandwiches and they weren't thinly sliced enough. Rye bread toasted. Last time, it wasn't toasted enough. Put the pickles, half sweet, half sour, on the side."

CARLO: When I went go to the deli, the owner waved me to the front of the line.

JOHNNY: You brought the fresh sandwiches to the bar, and they were made perfect. Everybody loved you.

Even then, I saw things in you. I saw that you could read situations and people at a young age. You were good with numbers and could remember things, which is why I chose you to go into gambling and being a bookie.

You're a good guy. You don't want to lose that.

You are coming out of your shell and gaining your self-confidence. Just remember to stay humble. I'm proud of you. You'll do the right thing.

I always looked at you as my kid. Stay good, I love you.

A lot of people talk about heaven and hell.

I know where I'm going.

I have a lot of friends down there, and I sent a lot of my enemies there too.

They will all be waiting for me.

You can put money on that.

I never did no good for nobody.

CARLO: You saved my life when I was a kid. You pulled me off the streets. I can't thank you enough for that.

JOHNNY: I didn't save your life. I ruined your life. I ruined Al's life. I ruined many lives.

Throw a torch at everything I taught you growing up. It was no good. I was no good.

CARLO: Don't say such things. They aren't true.

End of conversation dated December 24, 2015

Besides Johnny, the feds locked up other bosses and made guys.

This created a leadership void and chaos among the lower levels as these guys scrambled to take control of what was left.

The old-time bosses were gone and most of their rules and structure went away with them. This included the protection of the guys who earned income for the organization.

Now there was competition for who would "own" receiving the cash envelopes from each earner. I was an earner.

I felt like I was thrown to the wolves without protection.

The next week, three young guys coming up in the Salerno family waited in the fire escape at the end of the my condo hallway to ambush me.

I walked out of my elevator and down the hallway. I arrived at my door and unlocked it.

Once I cracked open the door, the guys shoved me in the back into the apartment.

I tripped and landed on the floor. I looked up disoriented at three guys standing over me.

One guy asked, "Where's your safe?"

Another began tying my hands and feet.

I adamantly howled, "Piss off, punks!"

One of them kicked me in the head. I blacked out for a moment.

One guy cracked open my safe in the bedroom and seized the $120,000 inside.

One stood over me and demanded, "From now on, you belong to us, your envelopes come to us, we'll be visiting you. Nobody else gets your envelopes.

If you have any problems, you come to us.

We make the rules now, do the right thing like you always have.

We own you and your operation.

Don't provoke us, we won't hesitate to come back, understood?"

I told them I understood. Being a good earner in the mob had its drawbacks. It was January 15, 2016.

THE VISIT

I didn't have any prior arrests so Johnny claimed I was his nephew and I visited him at Fort Dix, New Jersey prison.

January 15, 2016

JOHNNY: I feel like I am falling apart in here!

My prostate keeps getting bigger.

I get up 20 times a night to piss!

I am going nuts getting no sleep.

The doctors here want to zap part of my prostate with a laser to make it smaller so I can pee normal.

CARLO: The good news is you will get all of this fixed while you are in prison, so when you go home, you'll be a new man.

JOHNNY: I remember a saying my father told me when I was younger, "a broken plate, glued back together, is never the same."

I have been beat up, shot, banged up every which way in my life, but this prostate thing is the worst.

Every night at 8 o'clock, I start worrying.

Here we go again, up all night.

I can't take it!

I'm losing it!

I stay up almost constantly until 4 am in the morning, then I pass out and wake up at 5:30 am with piss all over myself!

CARLO: When do you get your prostate worked on?

JOHNNY: This Thursday, the surgery puts me out for a week. Then, five or six weeks after, everything should be normal.

Besides my health, I think a lot in here.

I see young guys struggling in here. I want to help them.

You take a guy who dropped out of high school to sell drugs on the street corners from the time he is twelve.

He gets arrested, prosecuted, and sent to jail, whip, bam, boom.

He gets a jail term of five to ten years.

He hangs out all day with other young guys just like him in jail, all day, every day.

What do you think they talk about?

They talk about the good old days in the neighborhood and how they can't wait to get back to doing what they used to do.

They talk about how they can improve their game so they can outwit the police next time.

They don't learn a thing about why they are here and how they should change the course of their life. This never bothered me before, but it bothers me now.

Even if a guy wants to get a job when he gets out, he receives no training while he is in jail.

No one learns any new skills.

And guess what?

The guys can't do anything else, but go back to drug dealing when he gets out. It is the only skill he has.

Welcome to wacky world!

CARLO: Can't they go work in a fast food restaurant? Those are everywhere.

JOHNNY: Can you believe some fast food restaurants don't hire felons?

These young guys are turned into second class citizens before they get started living their lives.

I hear it's still two out of every three guys who get released from jail end up coming back.

CARLO: Aren't the guys supposed to learn some type of lesson while they are in here?

JOHNNY: Learn a lesson? Ha! There is no learning going on here.

These guys have tough backgrounds. They come from poor families. I have heard some really tragic stories. Parents are drug addicts, dead or both.

CARLO: Sounds like me, but the only difference between my life and these young guys is at least you the took me in.

I can sympathize with the young guys here. I grew up on my own with little or no adult supervision, and I learned the rules of the streets.

I probably would have ended up the same as them if I didn't have you when I was coming up.

JOHNNY: Thanks. My point is the back and forth could be avoided.

For some of them, life is too good here, better than how they had it on the streets.

You might think, "Good? How could this possibly be too good?"

They get three free meals a day, they can watch cable TV with their friends, have free gym membership, use free medical care (even though it is mediocre), enjoy free heat, free electricity, free running hot water, and a clean dorm to live in.

I guess this makes it more difficult for them, in their own minds, to justify not coming back to jail.

The back and forth to jail cycle gets reinforced.

It's fruitless to bring this stuff up unless something can be done about it.

Look at us, here I am in prison talking about how to fix the prison system.

CARLO: What would you do if you had the power to change things?

JOHNNY: I would add skilled training like for electricians, plumbers, roofers, flooring, drywall, chef, landscaping, and other things like that. I would train them in jail so they could have a better chance at getting a legitimate job when they get out.

My work training programs would have to be attended by inmates with little or no job history.

A lot of these guys never had a job in their life, and many would push back to the training.

I wouldn't give them the choice. I would send them to solitary confinement if they refused.

There are no friends, no TV, no gym, no games, and no pool tables.

It is a room with one light bulb, a sink, toilet, concrete bed, and a shower. They get one hour outdoors a day.

CARLO: Is it possible to force guys to learn a skill?

JOHNNY: The government forces them to be in jail, don't they? This is just one more thing forced upon them.

I heard a statistic that 70% of guys who get out of jail end up unemployed.

I can see how this means eventually they go back to what they did before jail to earn a living.

If all a guy knows is how to be a drug dealer or criminal, then that is what he will return to being.

It's inevitable.

It's messed up.

Instead of training these guys, the government pays $32,000 a year per guy to incarcerate them, over and over, year after year.

CARLO: Now I understand one of the many reasons our government is in debt.

However, wouldn't it cost a lot more money to train these guys than just lock them up.

JOHNNY: I would hire more skilled tradesman to be on the prison staffs who could teach the inmates something of value and stop hiring unskilled staff who have very little to offer, except counting prisoners several times a day.

I never saw myself caring much about government and politics until I came to jail.

CARLO: Up until our visit today, I didn't give it much thought either. Unfortunately, you can't run for President after being locked up. Correct?

I feel bad for you being in here.

JOHNNY: Hey, I wasn't planning on slowing down at any point in my life. I would have been caught for any number of things.

Maybe you're thinking I would be visiting you in here rather than you visiting me?

If things worked out differently?

CARLO: Or we would be in here together.

JOHNNY: Things work out the way they do for a reason.

Over the years, I risked so much and have so little to show for it.

For many years, being a gangster was an endless adrenaline rush filled with fun and excitement.

I could do whatever I wanted.

I felt famous, financially comfortable and powerful.

I met interesting people, ate at the best restaurants, drove expensive cars, consumed the best drugs, attended exclusive parties, enjoyed vacations all over the world, sat in the best seats at the best shows and sporting events, and laughed more than I can remember.

Lots of people respected, idolized, and adored me.

Many people wanted to be my friend, or so I thought.

I heard that less than one percent of those who choose a criminal career avoid the legal or other consequences of such a choice.

I found this to be true because, whether or not they are aware of it, most everyone I know has either ended up in jail, is on their way back to jail, or, is dead.

Be a better man than I am.

Leave this life behind.

That is all I can hope for you going forward.

LIFE AFTER "THE LIFE"

May 2018 update from Carlo Juliano.

"I spent many years in the Salerno Crime Family of New York City, and now I am out.

Everything is different now, and my life will never be what it used to be.

I no longer fear for my life, and I don't carry two handguns to protect myself.

For most of my life, criminals surrounded me and they all wanted to know what I could do for them.

This included the endless scores bosses ordered me to do, the scores I helped others do, and the scores I came up with myself.

Over the years, I watched plenty of guys get locked up for crimes they committed, and their way of life led them to a twelve-man room, with all of their belongings in the world fitting in a 4' x 2' locker.

At the low security prison in Fort Dix, New Jersey, bosses and made guys live together as roommates.

They know everyone in their room because everyone is from the same neighborhoods in Brooklyn and Queens.

After they get out, they go back to the life they know. They try to stay one step ahead of the cops with their illicit activities, but fail.

They don't change with the times, they never learn, and they never grow.

They hold on to a life that is over, dead, and no more.